The History of Barnesville and Sellman Maryland

by
Dona Lou Cuttler
and
Ida Lu Brown

HERITAGE BOOKS
2008

HERITAGE BOOKS
AN IMPRINT OF HERITAGE BOOKS, INC.

Books, CDs, and more—Worldwide

For our listing of thousands of titles see our website
at
www.HeritageBooks.com

Published 2008 by
HERITAGE BOOKS, INC.
Publishing Division
100 Railroad Ave. #104
Westminster, Maryland 21157

Copyright © 1999 Dona Lou Cuttler and Ida Lu Brown

All rights reserved. No part of this book may be reproduced or transmitted in any form or by any means, electronic or mechanical, including photocopying, recording or by any information storage and retrieval system without written permission from the author, except for the inclusion of brief quotations in a review.

International Standard Book Numbers
Paperbound: 978-0-7884-1180-9
Clothbound: 978-0-7884-7287-9

ACKNOWLEDGMENTS

The Authors wish to express their appreciation to Elizabeth Hays Tolbert and Elsie Wood Pyles for their contributions and generosity. Special thanks also to Bob Lillard, William C. Hilton, Laura Bennett and Charles Knill. And for his continued support, photographs and expertise thanks to Michael Dwyer, Senior Park Historian, M-NCPPC. For their research members of the Regional Trails project, and to Jane Sween and Pat Anderson for information at the Montgomery County Historical Society thank you. For countless trips for land records, deeds and additional legwork, we are indebted to Mary Hertel. For numerous e-mails and checking facts, thank you Jane Parsley. For his heroic patience and tolerance for this project, and enduring the many questions, calls, and visits, thank you Richard P. Brown.

Table of Contents

Photographic Credits   vii

Chapter One   1
    The History of Barnesville

Chapter Two   25
    The Residences and Buildings

Chapter Three   107
    The History of Sellman

Chapter Four   111
    The Residences and Buildings

Bibliography   137

Index   139

Photographic Credits

Cover photo view of Sugarloaf Mountain, Brown Barn, D. Cuttler
Sketch of Battle for Sugarloaf, Harper's Weekly, October, 1862, p. 7
Sketch of Barnesville Encampment, A. R. Waud, October 25, 1862, p. 8
July 4, 1976, Ida Lu Brown, p. 11
Sugarloaf Cachet, D. Cuttler, p. 17
Time Capsule, Bonnie Brown, p. 21
Mayor Tolbert 250th Anniversary, 1997, Ida Lu Brown, p. 23
Barnesville Flag, D. Cuttler, p. 24
July 4, 1976, Ida Lu Brown, p. 24
Sketch of Tavern, collection of William Carr, p. 25
Sketch of Hotel, collection of William Carr, p. 26
Town Well, Montgomery County Historical Society, p. 26
Hays House, D. Cuttler, p. 27
Richard Poole, collection of Elizabeth Hays Tolbert, p. 28
Mary Poole, collection of Elizabeth Hays Tolbert, p. 28
Richard Poole Hays, collection of Elizabeth Hays Tolbert, p. 28
William O. Sellman, collection of Elizabeth Hays Tolbert, p. 28
Hays Clock, D. Cuttler, p. 29
Hays Mantle, D. Cuttler, p. 29
Hays Dining Room, D. Cuttler, p. 29
Barnes-Hays Cabin, collection of Elizabeth Tolbert, p. 30
Hays-White-Johnson House, Michael Dwyer, p. 31
Hays House, collection of Ida Lu Brown, p. 32
Hilton House, Michael Dwyer, p. 33
Barnesville Post Office, D. Cuttler, p. 34
Clagett Hilton House, Michael Dwyer, p. 35
Hilton Cabinet Shop, Connie Chesley, p. 36
St. Mary's Catholic Church, Montgomery County Historical Society, p. 37
Father Birch, Collection of St. Mary's Church, p. 40
St. Mary's Church, Ida Lu Brown, p. 40
St. Mary's Rectory, Markiewicz, p. 41
Parton House, D. Cuttler, p 42
Loy House, D. Cuttler, p. 43
Barn Hill, D. Cuttler, p. 44
Jeffers Farm, D. Cuttler, p. 45
Hays Farm, D. Cuttler, p. 46
Brown Tenant House, D. Cuttler, p. 47
Morningstar House, D. Cuttler, p. 48
Ryman Fire, Ida Lu Brown, p. 51
Hays Cemetery, D. Cuttler, p. 53
Brown House, collection of Tom Brown, 54
William Brown House, D. Cuttler, p. 55
Daybreak Farm, D. Cuttler, p. 56
John Brown Farm, collection of Richard P. Brown, p. 58
Kessler House, Michael Dwyer, p. 59

Offutt House, collection of William Hilton, p. 60
Morningstar House, D. Cuttler, p. 61
Offutt House, D. Cuttler, p. 62
Hersberger House, Michael, Dwyer, 63
Old Barnesville Store Sketch, artist unknown, p. 64
Stonestreet House, Michael, Dwyer, p. 65
Cecil House, D. Cuttler, p. 66
Voting Box, Paul C. Haller, 67
Pyles Store, J. R. Lillard, p. 68
Dixon House, D. Cuttler, p. 69
Boswell House, D. Cuttler, p. 70
Knott House, Ida Lu Brown, p. 71
Community Hall, D. Cuttler, p. 72
Cooley House, D. Cuttler, p. 73
Cooley House, Ida Lu Brown, p. 74
Clarence Brown House, Ida Lu Brown, p. 75
Charles Claggett House, Ida Lu Brown, p. 76
Garver-Menke House, D. Cuttler, 77
Ward House, Ida Lu Brown, p. 78
Ambush House, D. Cuttler, p. 79
Barnesville School, Montgomery County Historical Society, p. 81
Barnesville Baptist Church 1914, p. 84
Barnesville Baptist Church 1998, D. Cuttler, p. 84
Funk Farm, collection of Richard P. Brown, p. 85
Sellman House c. 1880, Montgomery County Historical Society, p. 86
Lawrence Hilton Price House, D. Cuttler, p. 87
Thomas Story House, Bonnie Brown, p. 88
Thomas O. White House, Bonnie Brown, p. 90
Barr House, Donald Barr p. 91
Hallman House, D. Cuttler, p. 91
William T. Hilton, collection of Ida Lu Brown, p. 92
Clagett C. Hilton, collection of Ida Lu Brown, p. 92
1903 Hilton Hearse, collection of William Hilton, 0. 93
Hilton's Funeral Home, collection of William Hilton, p. 93
Hilton House, D. Cuttler, p. 94
Burner House, Jane Parsely, p. 95
Erlich House, D. Cuttler, p. 96
Poole House, D. Cuttler, p. 97
Gott House, collection of George Miller p. 98
Hays House, D. Cuttler, p. 99
Mossburg House, Mrs. Gordon M. Smith, p. 100
Fink Farm, D. Cuttler, p. 101
Brewer House, D. Cuttler, p. 102
Noyes House, D. Cuttler, p. 103
Christ Episcopal Church, Ida Lu Brown, D. Cuttler, p. 104
Barnesville Post Office, D. Cuttler, p. 105
Wood House, collection of Hazel Wood Garvey Ochs p. 111

White-Fletcher House, D. Cuttler, p. 112
Telegraph office and Station, collection of William Hilton, 114
Barnesville Station, collection of Richard P. Brown, p. 115
Warfel's Store, D. Cuttler, p. 116
Frank Gibson House, D. Cuttler, p. 117
Dayhoff House, D. Cuttler, p. 118
Mt. Zion Parsonage, D. Cuttler, p. 119
Sellman School, collection of Dorothy Elgin, p. 120
Mt. Zion Church, D. Cuttler, p. 121
Sellman Community Center, MCHS, 122
Dorsett House, D. Cuttler, p. 123
Boot Leg Hill, D. Cuttler, p. 124
Glen Ellen, collection of Richard P. Brown, p. 125
Standard Oil Co., J. R. Lillard, p. 126
Sellman Store and Post Office, Michael Dwyer, p. 127
Pyles Store, Ida Lu Brown, p. 128
Sellman Post Mark, D. Cuttler, p. 128
Boyd House, Michael Dwyer, p. 129
John O. Pyles House, Ida Lu Brown, p. 130
Canning Factory, collection of Ann Cecil Morrison, p. 131
Factory House, collection of Ann Cecil Morrison, p. 132
William Washington Darby House, collection of Elsie Wood Pyles, p. 133
Knott Farm, Jane Parsley, p. 134
Darne House, D. Cuttler, p. 135
Mossburg House, D. Cuttler, p. 136

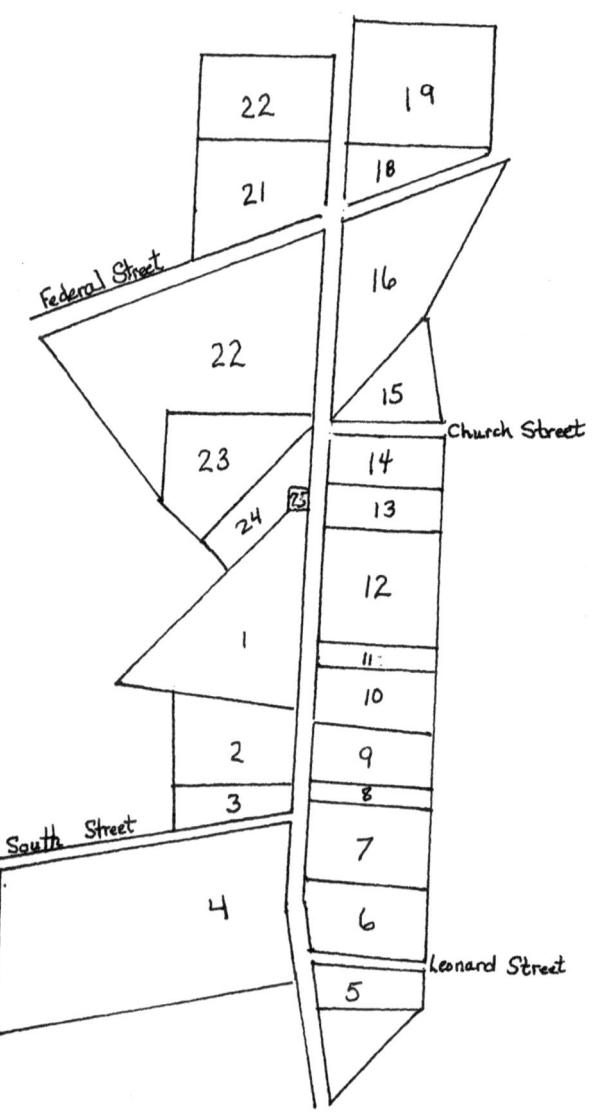

TOWN PLAT 1812

Chapter One

The land that became Barnesville was surveyed for Jeremiah Hays December 10, 1747. The tract "Jeremiah's Park" and "Hopson's Choice" were just two of the properties that eventually were surveyed as lots in the town. When the Baltimore Road was laid out it was first a dirt path from the Potomac River to Baltimore for the Loudoun and Prince George's County farmers to get their produce and stock to market. The following year, 1748, Frederick County was carved from Prince George's and the residents of the area were now in the newly formed county.

During the first ten years of growth along this section of the Baltimore Road a tavern was built and a livery stable was located nearby. Travelers stopped here overnight. On the crest of the hill James Barnes built a log house and operated his business here. Other early residents include Zachariah Knott, John Plummer and Captain James Gleeson.

In 1776 Montgomery County was created from Frederick County. One of the men from this area who served in the Revolutionary War was Captain James Gleeson. He also fought in numerous Indian offensives, and later fell to his death from the Monocacy aqueduct. Another local patriot was Lieutenant Colonel Edward Tillard who served in the 6th Maryland Militia from 1776-1779 under Colonel Otho Williams. In 1777 he was imprisoned at Staten Island, New York and later released. He then joined the 4th Maryland Militia from 1779-1781. After the war he was the saloonkeeper in Barnesville, and his daughter married Abram S. Hays.

James Barnes moved his family from Pipe Creek and purchased a parcel of land along the Baltimore Road. He was a shoemaker, and a Quaker. The village had a Catholic Mission, and a Methodist Chapel, but no Quaker Meeting House. After selling his land to Leonard Hays, in 1804 he packed up his belongings and left Barnestown, as it was then known. He and his brother David, Jr. moved their families to Ohio and laid out lots for a town, which was subsequently named for him.

A Roman Catholic Chapel had been established in 1741 as a mission of St. John's Church in Frederick. It served a parish that was spread over a large area. After much debate, it was decided to locate a new church building along the Baltimore Road. Zachariah Knott donated six acres and a frame church was constructed under the leadership of Father Plunkett. From Knott's acreage, timber for the building was cut, and Bernard O'Neil also donated lumber.

By 1808 there were several log houses in Barnestown, Sarah Claggett's, Zachariah Lloyd's, Leonard Hay's, a log store, tavern, a cobbler, blacksmith shop and livery stable. Jacob Stiers was the blacksmith, Benjamin Tucker kept the tavern and Father John DuBois was the priest.

Just out of town was a tannery run by John Poole, beginning in 1810. Later, Ira Elder was the tanner. This was located on the property which became the William O. Sellman farm. The town physician was Dr. Lisle. The second tavern keeper was William Trail, and the second merchant was John Plummer.

In 1811 several interesting advertisements appeared in the "Frederick Town Herald." On February 2 Thomas Reid was selling 141 acres of land three miles below Barnesville. On February 15 Samuel Spriggs sold 27 1/2 acres of land at a public auction held at Edward Tillard's Tavern in Barnesville.

The most significant event of 1811 was an Act of Assembly in November to have the town of Barnesville laid out and a survey of lots and streets recorded. Nathan Thomas Veatch was appointed to complete the survey. On July 24, 1812 George B. Hays delivered the town survey plot to recording clerk Upton Beall in Rockville. The cost was $3.13. George B. Hays, John Plummer and Abram Hays were the three town commissioners.

The following October Peter Hawkins placed an advertisement in the "Frederick Town Herald" offering a reward for a dark mulatto named Moses. Silas Ward was living in the house south of Captain Gleeson, and the next house was Frederick Nouse, furniture dealer. Nouse later moved to Keokuk, Iowa. The next two lots belonged to Magistrate Abram S. Hays, who held court in his parlor. His 250 acre farm was just outside the town limits. Opposite from the house was the blacksmith, where his slave "Old Ned" was the farrier.

Richard Gott purchased farm land that year, and William Sedwick advertised in the "Frederick Town Herald" for a journeyman blacksmith. At George McAtee's house an auction was held in November for the personal estate of Margaret McAtee.

William Sedwick must have found a journeyman blacksmith, for in the "Frederick Town Herald" of September 10, 1814 he placed the following advertisement "reward for return of Burgess R. Erp, apprentice, 20-21 years of age." That very day, local men were serving in the Battle of Bladensburg. Others were stationed in Frederick and Baltimore.

Also mentioned over the next few years in the "Frederick Town

Herald" as events in the village: December 2, 1815 William Hurley had a stray cow, February 3 there was a sheriff's sale at Mr. Murphy's tavern in Barnesville. William Warfield's 82 acres of "Conclusion" two miles from town were advertised by sheriff Arnold T. Winsor [sic]. The new "cash store" in Barnesville was operated by William Dougherty. He advertised in November 1816 that he had just received an assortment of dry goods, groceries, china, glass and queensware [flatware]. Also in November the tavern was the scene of another public auction for 986 acres of "Hope." The tavern keeper at this time was Joseph Talbott.

In May of 1817 520 acres near Sugarloaf Mountain were for sale by Edward Digges of Barnesville. On December 19, 1818 Jones left his horse at Talbott's Tavern without paying his bill. The post office was established on December 14 in the general store. Leonard Hays was the first town Postmaster. The Baltimore Road saw heavy traffic at this time. The farmers drove livestock toward Georgetown and Baltimore, and took produce in by wagons and carts. After harvesting their crop, large portions were taken to market, which brought the men through Barnesville.

Barnesville had one of the first schools in this part of the county. Abraham Simmons Hays built a school near his house just out of the town limits. It opened in 1819 and by 1830 had 100 pupils attending classes. In 1821 St. Mary's frame church caught on fire and although it was not destroyed, it was so badly damaged that the remaining section had to be torn down. Nearby, on the Monocacy River, the Chesapeake and Ohio Canal was under construction, as was the aqueduct. Many of the workers were brought from Ireland for their expertise in quarrying and masonry. In September of 1831 many succumbed to the cholera outbreak among the canal workers. So many were dying that the other workers buried the dead in the berm. Objections were raised about the Catholic workers not being in the church cemetery, so permission was obtained to bury 16 men at St. Mary's in Barnesville, in a common grave.

As the Chesapeake and Ohio Canal became a viable form of transportation, the type of traffic along the Baltimore Road slowly changed. By 1840 the businesses in town were not as prevalent, and Barnesville was no longer just a tavern stop for travelers. Residences were built, and a Methodist Episcopal Church was built. The Preacher-in-Charge during the construction was Randolph Richardson Murphy. The Society of Methodists had previously been worshipping in a log meeting house called "Bethel Chapel" on the property of Joseph Harris.

During the late 1850's the local men were interested in reorganizing the Maryland Militia with arms provided by the state. William O. Sellman organized the "Barnesville Guards" by January of 1861 with 47 members and musicians. Before the group was disbanded by the occupying Union forces later that year, Sellman stored a large quantity of arms and ammunition in his house. When his house was raided, the stash was found and the arms removed. Confederate Major William Mosby, "The Grey Ghost," nearly fell into Union hands as he planned to attend Mass at St. Mary's Church.

By this time William T. Hilton, local builder, had begun his prolific career. He was commissioned to build the new brick church at Sugarloaf, near present-day Comus, in 1861. Hilton purchased an exemption from the draft for $150 so that he could continue the project. Nearby in Poolesville, Major General Nathaniel Banks Division began their march to Frederick. The troops passed through Barnesville in December 1861.

Richard Poole Hays and four other Barnesville men joined Company B of the 35th Virginia Cavalry prior to the Maryland Militia's initiative to draft men in September of 1862. Meanwhile the Union forces in the area were on the move. General Franklin's Division was the next to come to town prior to the Antietam Battle. The following night Brigadier General John Joseph Abercrombie of Indiana set up temporary headquarters in the John Brown home in Barnesville during the march north. He placed guards around the house, as daughter Sallie recalled. The third night General Hamilton of Wisconsin made his headquarters at the same house; all three were Generals of Divisions. All of the regiments marching through Barnesville were pursuing Robert E. Lee's Army.

Lee hoped for Maryland to secede, and crossed at White's Ford to march toward Frederick. Sugarloaf Mountain was a natural choice for an observation point and opportunity for communications to be established. Signal guns were placed near the summit and small units of cavalry were dispersed to surrounding villages to screen the army's movements from General Robert McClellan, and for intelligence purposes. The townsfolk of Barnesville turned out to welcome the Southern troops and gladly provided food for the hungry soldiers.

General J. E. B. Stuart and his men arrived in early September to observe the enemy and slow their advance. A company of his men remained in Barnesville after he moved on and camped behind Mrs. William Clifton Brown's house. The soldiers lived off of hard tack which Mollie Hays Jones recalled hearing were as hard as bullets, only a different shape. Members of the company rigged up a "make believe" cannon from two front wagon wheels with a log propped on them. On September 9, the second week of the army's encampment, the residents were told to move into their cellars. At this time, cellars had dirt floors and some residents took blankets and mattresses with them. Stuart's men were preparing for battle, and the priest from St. Mary's blessed the men, many of whom were about to die.

It was the objective of the Confederate troops to gain control of Sugarloaf Mountain because of it's strategic location and importance to the nearby city of Washington and White's Ferry. On September 9, 1862 a bloody battle for control of the summit and town of Barnesville ensued. Because the Confederate forces considered this area of vital importance, they attacked the Union troops repeatedly. The town was taken by the Rebels and then retaken by the Army of the Potomac. The exchange of control fluctuated five times that day. Because the Confederate troops failed to gain complete control and access to the mountain, history books list the Union soldiers as the "winners."

The officers of J. E. B. Stuart's Company dined at the Hays House that night. The next day as Lieutenant Williams rode away with 17 men of the 7th Virginia Cavalry, he saw Colonel John F. Farnsworth with the 8th Illinois Cavalry and 3rd Indiana Cavalry advancing on the road to Poolesville, so he turned and headed for the mountain. Approximately one mile from Barnesville they were overtaken and the Lieutenant ordered his men to halt and give battle against an entire brigade.

Williams and Dr. Lacy were killed and are buried in the Methodist Cemetery. Four other men were seriously wounded and brought back to Dr. George W. Bowlen, the town doctor. Two of the wounded men soon recovered, and were taken to a Washington prison.

The wounded were given so much food by the neighbors, that the remaining portion was given to the doctor and his family. The ladies of Barnesville got up a subscription for the purchase of a new suit for the two remaining soldiers. One of them, Mr. Griffith, learned toward the end of October that he was to be taken away, so he walked out one Sunday afternoon to bid farewell to Mr. Lloyd Jones and thank him in person for the many kindnesses he had been shown. It was extremely hot, so Mr. Griffin, dressed in his new suit, found the walk of a mile there and back too much for him in his weakened condition. He died the next night, and was buried in his new suit, in the Methodist graveyard next to Dr. Lacy and Lt. Williams.

Mr. Ellis, the other soldier, stayed with Uriah Layton until the New Year, and then left in his new suit, still using his crutch.

New Year, and then left in his new suit, still using his crutch.

In October 1862, Stuart's troops were in Barnesville again, with 1800 men. From June 25-27 1863 the entire I and IX Corps, Army of the Potomac, passed through Barnesville after crossing the Potomac at Edward's Ferry en route to Gettysburg. The last time Barnesville saw the soldiers was in November 1864 when Barnesville served as Cavalry headquarters for the VIII Army Corps 1st Delaware Cavalry while they were stationed here to cover the fords.

During a 1940 interview Miss Sallie Brown recounted her memories of the war. Born on March 4, 1857 she lived in the 12 room Brown home were she made her living from doing handwork. Remembering the 1860's she says her father, a Union sympathizer, had to hide in haystacks outside of town when the "Rebs" came to Barnesville. She recalls that the soldiers feet were bare and bleeding, and that her mother bathed their feet in cool well water and gave them milk to drink. When the Yankees took control of the town, Major Thompson gave her mother a copy of the New Testament, which Miss Brown still had. Sallie tended her 140 chickens, and at the time of the interview was president of the Ladies' Guild of the Christ Episcopal Church, and former president of the Homemakers Club of Barnesville, Dickerson and Poolesville.

Men from Barnesville who served in Co B 35th Virginia Cavalry under General Rosser:
Sergeants: Henry Sellman, John Henderson, John Scholl, John Green
Privates: William Carlisle, David Carlisle, David Coberth, William Fitch,
    Richard Poole Hays, Samuel Brooke Hays, Abraham Harding,
    Benjamin J. Jones, Elias Moulden, Henry Orme, Lindly Orme,
    Richard Stallings, Martin Taylor

Union Troops Charging Ashbury's and Stewart's Cavalry. Barnesville

Encampment at Barnesville, 1862

By the end of the war in 1865 there were 35 buildings in Barnesville. This included two churches, two stores, a carpenter shop, blacksmith shop, and a school. That year the Barnesville Public School was chartered. Located on the road to Poolesville, the Barnesville Academy was used until it burned in 1871. Rebuilt on the same property, the contract was awarded to Nathan T. Talbott on March 17, 1874. The new building was 24 X 26 with a vestibule and was furnished with Soper's patented desks. Classes were held at this location until a new two room school was built in 1896. In 1929 the Barnesville Academy was torn down.

The following year William Hilton opened his cabinet shop where he also built coffins and operated an undertaking business. The community continued to grow during the post war years. The nearby Chesapeake and Ohio Canal was transporting coal and other goods to Georgetown, and St. Mary's became a separate parish, breaking away from Rockville. The Baptist church was also built in 1869 with 26 founding members. The Barnesville Academy burned down in 1871. It was rebuilt and re-opened in the same location.

Outlying land in the area was being purchased for a new branch of the Baltimore and Ohio railroad. The Metropolitan Branch would provide service from Point of Rocks to Washington with a stop near Barnesville. This section was under the supervision of James A. Boyd. As land was condemned for the laying of the tracks, farms were divided. Construction camps for the workers were put up and the population boomed, temporarily.

Train service began in 1873 to Barnesville Station, now called Sellman. A station was built and a commercial district followed soon after this. The railroad shifted the transportation focus from the canal to a faster, more economical way to get products to market. From livestock to milk, the farmers could move higher volumes via the Metropolitan Branch.

A Barnesville tradition began on July 26, 1875 with the annual Catholic Church picnic. Over the years the picnic has changed from a family event to include a large gathering of visitors. Formerly, dinners were served in the picnic woods, beyond the pavilion at St. Mary's. Chickens were fried in iron skillets on kerosene stoves. Parishioners brought home made pickled beets, cole slaw, corn, potato salad, succotash, and baked goods. But now, large barbecue pits replace the iron skillets and other food is prepared in a health department approved kitchen to serve thousands. Jousting tournaments thrilled the crowds, as riders attempted to snatch rings on their spears while riding their horses at breakneck speed. With each round, smaller, and smaller rings were hung, and less steady riders were winnowed out. Locals bet on the skilled riders. In 1938 the jousting was done on bicycles. The jousting tournament took place in the morning, and people from neighboring communities came to spend the day. Ladies in regal costumes were paraded on the horses. Bingo was called by Lloyd Jones, and later by the Hiltons. Prizes included toys, tools, dishes and household items. The cake stands were always popular, with the wheel spinning to announce the lucky winner. Penny pitch was a favorite among the children, as they had saved all year for the picnic. Prizes included canes, fuzzy animals, balls and candy. The Poolesville Band, led by Mr. Walter Matthews, and comprised of many of his own family, was hired to play for the evening dances which were held in the pavilion. The pavilion used to have large windows that swung down on hinges for light and air. Around the walls were wooden benches where the wallflowers sat, and the windows were covered with wire. The pavilion was enlarged in the 1940's and a kitchen was added at that time. Food for the picnic is now prepared in the county health department approved facility, and the chickens come from a poultry market. The dance is no longer held, and meals are served in the dining room of the pavilion.

By 1879 the population of Barnesville was 175. This included merchant Richard P. Hays, blacksmith Charles W. Miles, wheelwright Nathan E. Miles, carpenter William T. Hilton, undertaker Allen S. Orme, hotel keepers W. H. Carr and Nathan J. Talbott, millers John W. Darby and R. R. Darby, physicians George W. Bowlen and Robert Vinton Wood and shoemaker Charles S. Nichols.

The citizens of Barnesville formed an agricultural society in 1882 and founded the Grange in 1883. They built the Grange Hall, a two-story frame building across from the pavilion at St. Mary's.

Barnesville had been laid out in 1812, 76 years prior, when in 1888 it was incorporated. Elections were held on May 7 and the bylaws were written and adopted June 11, 1888. The first election judges were Nathan T. Talbott, Leonard I. Hays and John W. Brown. The ballots were cast in a Perfection Cigar box, still in use today. The results were: Dr. Robert Vinton Wood, president; Thomas Story, clerk; Charles W. Miles, bailiff; William T. Hilton and Charles S. Nichols.

A tax rate was set and ten ordinances were passed by the commissioners. The town was dry [no hard liquor] and blue laws were enforced [Sunday observance laws]. The first town tax collection yielded $44.72 plus $7.00 in dog tax. Commissioner Hays was authorized to repair gutters from the house of Richard Pyles to the Mountain Road. The original ordinances prohibited careless riding or driving in the streets, litter such as grass, garbage, wood or any other obstruction on the streets or sidewalks, the use of profanity, the keeping of any pig-sty, stable, cow house or dung heap near the streets or in places to impair the health or comfort of citizens; livestock running loose, destruction of any shade tree, destruction of commissioner notices, and an annual dog tax of $1.00 on males, $2.00 on females over 6 months. The following paid a dog tax in 1888: John Coughlin, William T. Hilton, Mrs. Julia Loy, Oliver S. Maus, Elisha Miles and Solomon Plummer. Commissioner Leonard I. Hays proposed a ban on liquor sales and businesses operating on Sunday. The town commissioners proposed sidewalks, and 6000 feet of board was delivered from the mill of G. A. and F. A. Zeigler. Francis Knott, John Brown and Leonard Awkard built the sidewalks which consisted of a base layer of broken stones hauled by Nathan Talbott. Boards were nailed to support pieces to form a wooden sidewalk. Three foot walks were built along South Street from Dr. Wood's house on the corner to the Episcopal Church woods. Also, two foot walks were laid from the Methodist Church on Main Street to Luther Cecil's house. John Brown was directed to keep the leftover lumber until the following year. Other business included cleaning ditches, and issuing liquor ordinances to ban the sale of cider.

JULY 4, 1976

1888 Tax list:

	Real Estate	Personal	Total	Tax
Barnesville Grange		500		.50
Dr. Geo. W. Bowlen	1400	445	1845	1.85
John W. Brown	1962	895	2857	2.86
John T. Carlin	150		150	.15
Luther Cecil	1000	400	1400	1.40
Charles Claggett	250		250	.25
John Coughlin	200		200	.20
			dog	2.00
Annie Donn & Mrs. Getzendanner				
	160		160	.16
Sarah Eagle	700	200	900	.90
			dog	1.00
Fred P. Hays	30		30	.03
Leonard Hays		300	300	.30
Leonard I. Hays	2000	615	2615	2.62
Richard P. Hays	1600		1600	1.60
Samuel S. Hays	1250	1035	2285	3.39
Clagett C. Hilton		150	150	.15
William T. Hilton	1000	200	1200	1.20
			dog	1.00
John Jones	200		200	.20
Alexander Jamison		400	400	.40
Mrs. Mary Jane Knott	1000	200	1200	1.20
Mrs. Julia Loy		150	150	.15
			6 dogs	6.00
James Manion		150	150	.15
Oliver S. Maus		250	250	.25
			dog	1.00
Elisha Miles		200	200	.20
			dog	1.00
Nathan E. Miles	1050	150	1200	.15
Charles S. Nichols	300	150	450	.45
Allen S. Orme	600	150	750	.75
Mrs. E. L. Poole	600		600	.60
Mrs. Priscilla J. Poole		3240	3240	3.24
Solomon Plummer	1200	300	1500	1.50
			dog	1.00

Isaac J. Pyles	750	1500		2250	2.25
Richard T. Pyles	2770	4000		6770	6.77
Mrs. Wilhelmina Sherman	300			300	.30
Thomas Story		250		250	.25
Nathan T. Talbott	4000	750		4750	4.75
Millard Whalen	100			100	.10
Mrs. Hulda A. White	400			400	.40
Mrs. Mary E. White	1300	300		1600	1.60
Dr. R. Vinton Wood	700	500		1200	1.20
Total	dogs $13.00	$48.33			

In 1889 the sidewalk was extended from Pyles store northward to Frank Knott's gate. The dog tax law was re-written to allow each family to have one dog tax-exempt. The following year the ladies of Barnesville raised money for five street lamps, the town commissioners appropriated the money for a sixth, six posts and the cost of installation. Richard Alonzo Rice dug the holes for the lights the following year and Bailiff Benjamin F. Roberson was to keep the lamps lit, filled, cleaned and in good repair.

In 1891 Samuel S. Hays, Justice of the Peace, began holding court in his parlor. In 1893 Richard Alonzo Rice was appointed Bailiff. In 1895 Kiernon Manion was the magistrate. The Barnesville Academy was 22 years old when a new public school site was purchased for $50.00 from Frederick and Ida Hays. The new school was built closer to the center of town, on the corner of Stove Street and Main Street. Wooden side walks were laid as far as the school that year. A fire destroyed Nathan Talbott's tavern in 1894. In 1898 Professor Thomas Story was appointed town clerk at $10.00 per annum.

The new century in Barnesville began on a sad note. St. Mary's Church burned, and the congregation began plans for the new building. William T. Hilton was hired to build a brick church near the site of the old building, but closer to Main Street. Following this, the General Assembly repealed the act of incorporation and there were no more elections in Barnesville for four years.

In 1904 the act of incorporation was reinstated and the town boundaries were changed. The number of town commissioners was changed from five to three. Clagett C. Hilton, Thomas O. White and Luther E. Cecil were elected. Thomas Story was the clerk and treasurer and he served until his death March 5, 1914. The sidewalks were repaired and the following year mud holes in front of the parsonage were filled with crushed stone. Over the next few years the commissioners were busy with ordinances such as horses and vehicles were forbidden on sidewalks, no ball playing in the street, citizens were forbidden to injure or destroy trees, and no stock running at large in the streets. These were posted in the post office, located in the store. The first telephone poles were planted in 1909. A party line for Hilton's, Miss Sallie Brown, the Hays' and Lillard's store was installed. The ring for the Hays house was one-one. Pipes were installed under Main Street to convey surplus water. Main Street was then graded, and crushed stone was laid. Also, dog tags were issued in 1909:

		tag #
John W. Brown	Caper	11
Mrs. Cunningham	Bingo-died	8
Charles R. Darby	Billy Bryan	3
Fred Jones	Shep	12
Zack Loy	Fido	14
Kiernon Manion	Rover	9
Lawrence Price	Jack	6
Percy Pyles	Tuck	1
Dr. Stonestreet	Jack	5
Thomas O. White	Billy-died	23

It was in 1912 that concrete sidewalks were under construction, a project of Clagett C. Hilton and Charles R. Darby. Speed limit signs were ordered for Main Street. In 1914 sidewalks were installed from Grange Hall to the Methodist Church. Dr. Joseph White purchased the Wade House and opened a maternity hospital upstairs. He also had an office on the ground floor. In 1915 the commissioners were Charles T. Brosius, W. C. Brown, and Dr. Joseph White. In 1917 when the United States entered World War I some of the Barnesville men who served were: John "Chalk" J. Johnson, Dr. Leonard Hays, Patrick McDonald, Green Poole and Bryan Barr.

Due to the 1918 influenza epidemic the town commissioners passed an ordinance prohibiting the establishment of institutions which would provide care to individuals afflicted with communicable diseases. The town commissioners in 1918 were: Charles T. Brosius, William C. Brown and Charles Darby.

In 1920 James Robert Lillard operated a general store, which he ran for the next 20 years. The post office was housed here during this time period. Mrs. Lillard served as the postmaster while Herbert Dixon was serving in the army. At the Baptist parsonage Rev. J. C. McFadden's stable yard entrance was ordered to be piped. In the 20's all the area towns had baseball teams, The Hays Boys made up the team and practiced with John "Chalk" Johnson. Once when a team member was absent, they substituted Chalk and the visiting team refused to play, and forfeited the game. From then on Chalk played and Barnesville is credited with having the first integrated area team.

The town decided to have a community hall built to hold their socials and entertainments. The citizens of Barnesville raised funds toward building the hall and Mrs. Lonnie Hilton deeded property to the Trustees in 1925 for $10.00. The frame building had a stage for plays and for a while the annual fall turkey dinners were held here, a St. Mary's fund raiser. The Trustees were Clagett C. Hilton, J. Forrest Gott, F. Leonard Hays, Milton Phillips, and Arthur C. Hersberger. "To procure, own or provide a hall for social intercourse, entertainments, public meetings of religious, political, or social nature." Elections were held here after the grange was no longer usable.

In 1927 there was a surplus of cash on hand and the commissioners decided to put in six additional street lights, bringing the total to 12. The following year the commissioners were: William B. Hilton, William C. Brown and James Robert Lillard. In 1931 Potomac Edison installed lights in the community hall at a cost of $125.00. In 1933 Clagett C. Hilton died, and William B. took over well drilling and the funeral home business. The commissioners decided to pay $294.12 toward the debt on the Community Hall, reducing the principle to $1,000.00.

In 1937 the converted tavern was purchased to house coal which had been hauled from western Maryland by Mr. Lillard's trucking business employee's. The coal was delivered to homes and businesses for heating. Esso gasoline was sold at the store during this time period. Potomac Edison installed five new incandescent street lights in 1939. Citizens who had lights in front of their house were assessed to pay $9.00 monthly, but this was later reversed and the residents were reimbursed. In 1940 the old school was sold to Arthur and Helen Bready who renovated it for a residence.

Some of the Barnesville men and women who served in World War II were: E. L. "Tip" Lillard, Charles "Sex" Orme, Tom Kessler, Carol Moomaw, Lawrence H. "Buddy" Price, Herbert T. Dixon, Joseph N. Starkey, Jr., George Barr, Randy Luhn, Tom Morningstar, Jim Darby, Col. Carl Von Dem Busche, Harold Ryman, Rosalyn Hersberger, John Stowers, William Poole, Benton Jeffers, Paul Jeffers, Donald Jeffers, Richard Jeffers, Mark Jeffers, Joseph Harris Stonestreet, Jr. and Col. Sam

Tolbert. Bobby Lillard and Frederick Sprigg Hays served in the Korean War.

In 1942 shipping pallets were made in Hilton's cabinet shop. Six to eight locals were employed, one was Albert Hawse. In the 1946 elections a woman candidate was elected for the first time as a commissioner of Barnesville, and although Mary Morningstar received the most votes, R. S. Hays was chosen as president, and L. Jerome Offutt served as third commissioner.

1946 saw the installment of an additional party line in Barnesville. Now less families were sharing phone service, but there was still room for improvement. Mary Morningstar was elected president of commissioners the following year. Trash collection service began in 1949. In 1951 Ida Lu Price was commissioned as the twenty-second postmaster of Barnesville, by Postmaster General Jesse M. Donaldson on the 26th of June. The first annual Barnesville Community Christmas Tree was decorated in 1954 on the site of the former tavern. As a result of an increase in the volume of mail, Barnesville's post office was promoted from 4th class to 3rd class Post Office in July of 1963. That was also the year that "Lilith" was filmed starring Warren Beatty. The jousting sequence was shot in Barnesville, in the picnic woods behind St. Mary's Church. Many of the extras in the scenes were Barnesville citizens and the town received $300.00 a day from the film company for the use of the streets and clean-up after the horse scenes. Some of the locals spotted in the final version were: Jack Cooley, Doris Matthews, Jane Price, Mary Knill, Jerome Offutt and Archie McGaha.

The first "Barnesville Day" was held in 1968. Designed to be a family reunion for the local families, it is now an annual dinner held in November, and more of a town gathering these days. Also that same year the Barnesville General Store closed. But new homes have added to the community, such as the Todd and June Barr Luhn house, the Ralph Cooley, Jr. house, the Notley Davis house, the Charles and Barbara Ward house, the Easter cabin, the Deaner and Margaret Lawless house, the Earl Shreve house, the Paul and Carol Erlich house and the Barton and Ella Atwood house. The Conoy development began in the late 1960's.

On July 1, 1971 the Barnesville Post Office marked "Postal Service Day." Mayor George T. Wood presented Postmaster Ida Lu Price with a proclamation on June 29 1971 proclaiming July 1, 1971 as Postal Service Day. Customers of Barnesville were invited to stop in for refreshments provided by Comus Homemakers Club.

Parking at the post office had been a problem in the community since automobiles appeared in town. Ida Lu Price purchased the abandoned house next door to the post office, had it removed and paved the lot for parking, thus ending 20 years of illegal parking in front of her house.

The largest event in Barnesville, the annual St. Mary's picnic, celebrated it's 100th anniversary on July 26, 1975. The following year, Barnesville was officially declared a Bicentennial Community and celebrated the United States 200th Birthday with a parade and other activities.

Ida Lu Price received best handling of a news story in "Free State Postmaster" for her article on rural delivery in winter weather in Garrett County, Maryland in 1977. In 1980 Elizabeth Tolbert was elected as mayor of Barnesville. In 1983 Retired Barnesville Postmaster Ida Lu Brown suggested Sugarloaf Mountain to represent Maryland's cachet entry in the National Association of Postmasters of the United States. The subject that year was "One of the most important natural or man-made wonders in the state." A limited edition of 1,000 were issued and hand canceled "Dickerson, MD."

1987 was the the year that the 1862 Battle of Barnesville for Sugarloaf Mountain was reenacted. The following year, for the 100th Anniversary of Incorporation, Judge Noyes submitted the town motto "A Caring Community." In 1990 Barnesville was designated a Rural Village, one of only 10 communities so named in Montgomery County. On October 4, 1998 a time capsule was buried containing the names of the current residents, photos, momentos and articles about Barnesville. The annual turkey dinner was held on October 31, 1998. The mayor and residents are hard at work to keep the town "A Caring Community."

SUGARLOAF CACHET

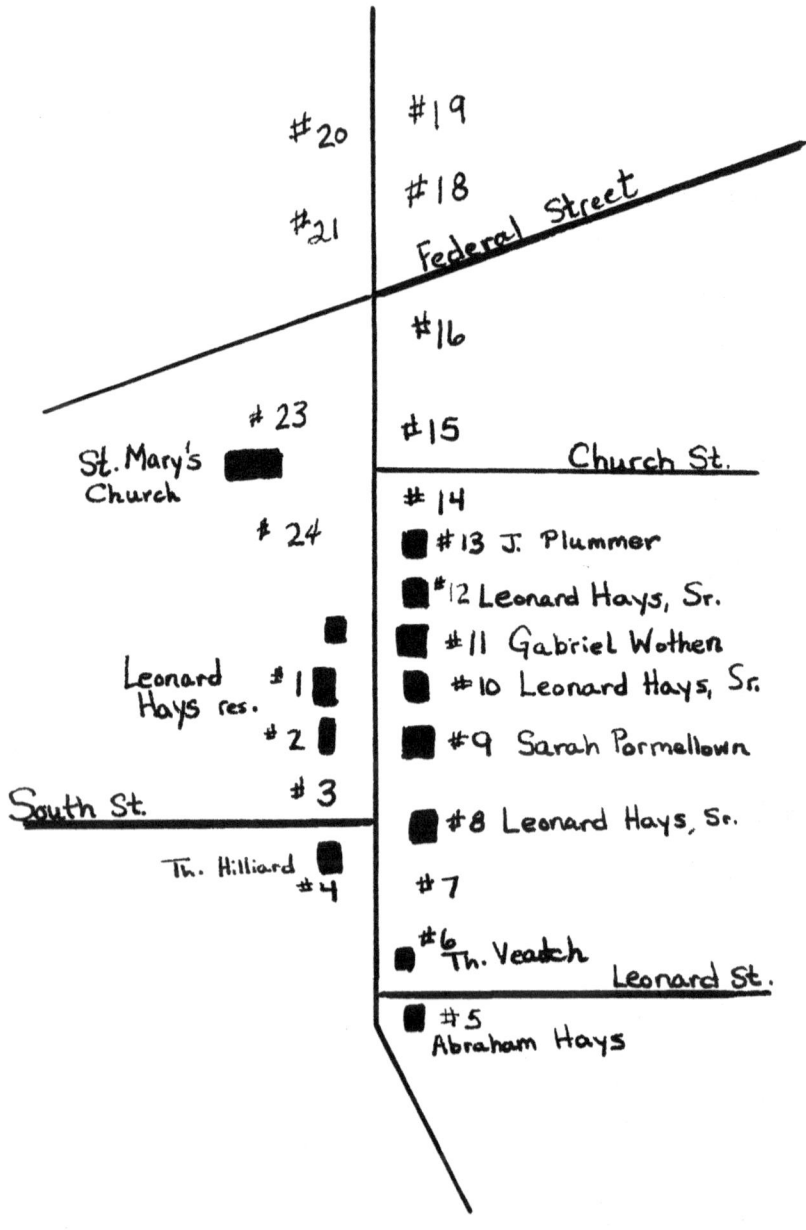

TAX ASSESSMENT 1822

POSTMASTERS AT BARNESVILLE

William S. Hayes	14 Dec 1818
No one listed	1819
Leonard Hays, Jr.	1822 Name changed to Barnesville 1830
William S. Hays	1833
Leonard Hays, Jr.	27 May 1835
William D. Poole	15 Mar 1837
Leonard Hays, Jr.	14 Apr 1847
Samuel S. Hays	30 Jun 1849
Leonard Hays, Jr.	19 Jan 1855
John C. Gott	11 May 1860
John W. Brown	16 Aug 1865
Richard T. Pyles	1872-1888
F. E. Pyles	1889-1898
Allen S. Orme	1899-1907
John W. Brown	1907-8
Sallie E. Brown	1909
Gertrude W. Gough	4 Dec 1926
William C. Bean	27 Aug 1934, 4th class
Emily Darby Brown	11 Jun 1935
Herbert Dixon	25 Jan 1938
Stella Lillard	5 Sep 1941
Edna P. Titus	10 Jul 1944
Evelyn D. Matthews	13 Jun 1945
Herbert T. Dixon	14 Sep 1945
Evelyn D. Matthews	24 Jan 1947
Ida Lu Price	14 Jun 1951
Mary Loretta Offutt	1976
Maureen Webster	12 Mar 1988

In 1951 there were 35 box holders, mail was delivered four times daily by mail messenger from the train at Sellman. There were 65 boxholders by 1973 with 20 delivery customers. Mail was delivered twice daily via truck Star Route from Rockville. In 1965 the Barnesville Post Office was changed from 4th class to 3rd class. The post office was moved to various locations depending on the business or residence of the postmaster.

Postal Patrons 1879

Frederick Bowman
J. F. Cooley
Zachariah G. Cooley
J. W. Darby
A. S. Harris
S. F. Harris
Frederick P. Hays
L. J. Hays
Christian R. Hershey
William Hodges
Charles Lawman
James Lawman
Frederick Linthicum

John H. Lynch
James Pearre
Algernon Poole
W. N. Reid
L. L. Sellman
John P. Sellman
William O. Sellman
W. W. Wade
Thomas H. Ward
Richard G. White
William B. White

Postal Patrons 1949

3 A. L. Vorhees
4 Charles C. Orme
5 Albert Easter
6 E. Wilson Jordan
7 Harold G. Stottlemyer
8 Spencer Fisher
11 Algie T. Morningstar
12 William H. Warren
13 Mark P. Jeffers
14 Sallie E. Brown
15 Rev. Philip J. Brown
16 Hatton D. Brown
17 Robert L. Haller
18 George F. Cooley, Jr.
21 James Wilson
22 Herbert J. Kessler
23 Richard Shirley Hays

24 Carlton G. Van Emon
25 William B. Hilton
26 James Robert Lillard
27 Victor Manion
28 Stephen Newton Brewer
31 E. M. Gleason
32 Richard P. Brown
33 Lawrence H. Price
34 Edgar Morningstar
35 Charles Garrett Cooley
36 Mrs. A. C. Hersberger
37 James Henry Ambush
38 Harold F. Cooley

Frontage Measurements in 1888   Main Street North Side

Charles S. Nichols
Methodist Episcopal Church
J. T. Carlin   Road to Poolesville: east
Mrs. Wilhelmina Shearman   Nathan T. Talbott
John W. Brown   Allen S. Orme
Dr. George Bowlen   John Coughlin
Samuel S. Hays   John Jones
Richard T. Pyles   School House
Isaac J. Pyles
Solomon Plummer
Mary White
Richard P. Hays   West side:
Luther E. Cecil   Dr. R. V. Wood
Richard T. Pyles   Leonard J. Hays
Mrs. Mary Jane Knott   Christ Episcopal Church
Hays heirs
Isaac J. Pyles
Frederick P. Hays
Baptist Church

250TH ANNIVERSARY TIME CAPSULE 1997

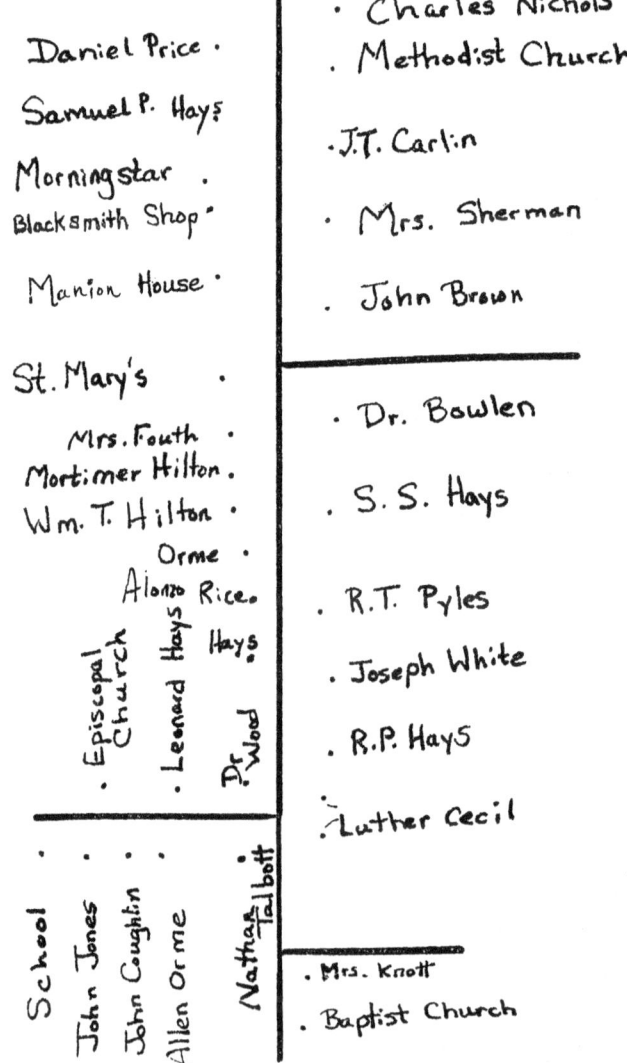

TOWN PLAT 1888

SUGARLOAF MOUNTAIN

Sugarloaf Mountain rising over the plains,
Rising over farms and full of grains.
Watching over small towns, all the year round,
She sits there so proudly, not making a sound.

She has lots of memories of battle and war,
Of cannons and gunfire, which side was she for?
She remembers Indians, in some of the woods,
Living by rivers, traveling by foot.

But now times have changed and wilderness no more,
No Indians or soldiers, or battles or war.
But how I do love her, rising over the plains,
Rising over farms and fields full of grains.

Daniel Benson January 17, 1976 age 12
used by permission

250th Anniversary in 1997, Mayor Tolbert

The Barnesville Flag was designed to commemorate Maryland's 350th Anniversary by Julia Jeffers, William D. Hilton, Robert Lillard, Dalis Miller and J. Robert Stonestreet. Dedicated in a ceremony at the Barnesville Baptist Church, it features the town well with Sugarloaf Mountain in the background.

July 4, 1976

Chapter Two
Residences and Buildings

1. Grove Hotel and Tavern

On the corner of Main Street and the road to Beallsville several structures occupied lot #3. The oldest was the tavern and Grove Hotel where John Hilton was one of the saloonkeepers. An ice house was also on the property. In the next lot, facing Main Street, was the Mary Jones House. Additionally, a residence was on the property by 1887 facing the road to Beallsville, in which Dr. Wood lived. The well which was dug by hand remains. At a later date, a part of the tavern was being used as a store and part was a residence. Coal was stored in the building after being delivered by rail and before it was delivered to area homes. David Cole was renting the back portion of this building in 1937 when Mr. Lillard purchased the property to build a garage in which to store his trucks. He changed his mind after the building was torn down and built adjacent to his home. When the building was being torn down in 1938 Mr. Lillard found the old tavern fares listed in pence and pounds painted on the wall. Unfortunately, the list was not preserved. In the 1940's the well was refurbished by Thomas W. Brown, local stone mason. The water was later declared unfit for human consumption and the well was capped in the 1960's.

Grove Hotel

Town Well

2. Leonard Hays House

The Hays family purchased land in this area in 1747. In 1822 they owned over a thousand acres in and surrounding Barnesville. Also they ran the store, owned the blacksmith shop, and other enterprises. According to the 1850 census Leonard Simmons Hays, former proprietor of the general store across the street, farmer and postmaster, owned many lots in Barnesville, and lived at this home, the geographical center of the town. By the late 1880's this house on lot #1 was infested with termites and the front section was rebuilt by William Hilton, who completed it in 1890, after Leonard I. had his father's house razed. Many notable men were entertained here including J. E. B. Stuart, Daniel Webster's son Col. Fletcher Webster, and Col. W. H. F. Lee. The frame addition to the mid-eighteenth century rear section, shows Hilton's ability to fuse various styles and construction techniques. The Hilton woodworking mill was close by and supplied lumber for the building, which features a curved stairway and rail, marble mantels, plaster ceiling ornaments and heavy wood trim on the doors and window openings. The clock pictured below was made by a German clock maker working in Frederick. Other interesting furnishings include the ship's table in the hall, passed down in the Hays family from Captain Wailes from the War of 1812, a Chippendale mirror and period dining room suit. Mayor Elizabeth Hays Tolbert is the fifth generation of this family to live here.

Richard Poole

Mary Poole

Richard Poole Hays

William O. Sellman

Hays Clock

Hays Mantel

Hays Dining Room

3. site of James Barnes Cabin

James and Ann Barnes sold their German style log house on two acres in 1803 to Leonard Hays. They packed up and moved to Belmont County, Ohio. In 1812 this property became part of lot #1. John Kinder sold the property in 1816 to George Reid who subsequently sold it to Joseph A. Murphy. Later occupants include John Poole, Thomas Poole, John Pearre, William Hays and Richard Alonzo Rice. Maurice Ricketts lived here until 1939, after which the house was torn down. The house had been partially clapboarded over, was one and a half stories with a steeply pitched A roof which extended over the porch too.

4. Hays-White-Johnson House

Inherited by Leonard Hays, Jr. from his father in 1822, this is one of the oldest houses in Barnesville. The log section predates the town's founding and was built on a fieldstone foundation. Part of lot #1, the frame section was added later and clapboarding updated the house during one of the renovations. It passed to his daughter, Ellen Hays Poole in 1864, but in 1878 Richard Gott White was living there. The Poole heirs sold it to Clagett C. Hilton in 1929. After his death in 1933, the house remained in the family. While Harold G. "Newt" Stottlemyer was working for the Hiltons, his family lived here in the 1940's, followed by Robert Haller. The house was sold to Edwin Johnson in 1964. David Johnson purchased the house in 1974 and has remodeled it recently.

5. Mary Alice Hays House

Built c. 1880 on a parcel of lot #24 by William T. Hilton, this house had a brick first floor with frame on the second story, center gable, three bays and a center door with front porch. Maurice Orme, son of Allen, lived here until his death. He ran a watch repair business from the adjoining shop. Harry and Gigi Ward lived here in the 1950's. It was then a rental property until it was repossessed by Damascus Bank and sold to Ida Lu Brown. In 1972 the lot was deemed too small to accommodate a sewer and the well, the house had been condemned, so it was demolished. The lot then became a parking lot for the post office, which was located next door at that time. Later, the lot was sold to David Johnson.

6. William T. Hilton House

The original log section of the house dates from 1835 when John Poole, Sr. purchased the property from William S. Hays. John Hilton, shoemaker, purchased the property in 1847 from William Fischer when it was still lot #24. William T. Hilton returned to Barnesville from apprenticing in Mouth of Monocacy and brought his family to live here in 1866. In 1867 John turned the property over to his son William with life tenancy rights. William T. Hilton, builder, progressed from the Italianate style to Victorian, as evidenced in his work throughout the area. The house was conveyed to Jessie Hilton Price, then to Lawrence Hilton Price, and then to his son. Jack Cooley, Sr. and the Titus family were among the tenants during the time the house was rented out. The 1900 addition to the house later served as the post office from 1952 until 1990. Letters were hand-canceled, and patron's boxes were located in the converted parlor. The 1945 renovations added plumbing, electrical rewiring, and other conveniences. The original kitchen was removed and a family room added, built with local lumber by Lawrence Price and his son Lawrence, Jr.

Barnesville Post Office 1910-1974

7. Clagett Hilton House

In 1863 John Hilton and Nathan Talbott sold this parcel of lot #24 to James F. and Fanny E. Fitch. This property had two small houses, one owned by Joel H. and Annie Mary Wolfe, who bought 76 perches from Fitch. The two houses can be seen in the sketch on page seven. This property was sold to Nathan and George Miles when the Wolfes moved to Comus. By 1878 Dr. Bowlen owned this house. In the other house occupants included Mrs. T. V. Fouth, and later Mortimer Hilton. In 1891 these properties were combined when William T. Hilton purchased them from Lycurgus and Sarah Eagle, and Mortimer Hilton. The present house was built c. 1903, for Clagett C. Hilton, who was involved with laying the concrete sidewalks in 1912-1913. He also was a cabinet maker, well driller and undertaker. Marjory Cordova Byrd purchased the house in 1965. She raised her family here and sold the house in 1985 to Paul and Maureen Webster, the current postmaster. Glen Beagle lives here now.

8. Hilton Cabinet Shop

William T. Hilton traveled to building sites with portable tools and used local timber for buildings. Much of the decorative and ornamental finishing work was done at this site part of lot #23, where lathes, planing and other tools were available. The stairs had rollers on them for moving caskets and heavy furniture. Joists and beam lumber were cut on Sugarloaf Mountain, and farmers who were clearing land with a hatchet often sold lumber by the cartload to Hilton for use in his construction of homes. In the mill he employed the Orme brothers, and Mr. Ambush. Mr. Ambush earned twenty-five cents a day to turn the lathe. Steam power was introduced around 1900. The Orme brothers were paid by the day at $1.25 and when Hilton was paid by the day, he got $2.00. Most jobs were by commission, and he built approximately 10-12 houses a year, according to William C. Hilton. The undertaking business grew out of the carpentry business, as it mainly entailed building plain, wooden coffins.

9. St. Mary's Catholic Church

St. Mary's Church was originally a mission of St. John's Church in Frederick. A chapel was established in "Barnestown" in 1741. In 1807 Father John Dubois proposed building a church in Barnesville. Zachariah Knott gave eight acres of land, and Bernard O'Neil donated the lumber. The building was 50 feet long and 28 feet wide. The church was plastered and painted, and featured 40 pews. It was dedicated in 1808 by Father Dubois. When the town was surveyed this property became lot #23. The frame church building pictured below had 160 members by 1813. The interior of the church was finally completed in 1869 under Father Joseph Birch, the first resident pastor of the church. On July 14, 1900 the church was destroyed by fire.

The contract for the new church was awarded to William T. Hilton. The parish borrowed $2,500 and donated their time and teams of horses to begin rebuilding their church. The cornerstone was laid by Rev. Gilbert H. McDonald. Rev. John Gloyd of St. Patrick's Church officiated, Rev. M. J. Riordan, former pastor, gave the homily. The brick Victorian Gothic Church cost $9,000 to build and is 40 feet by 70 feet. The steeple is 12 feet square and is 77 feet high, topped by a six feet high gold cross. Bricks for the construction were ordered by Hilton from Williamsport and towed down river to Dickerson, where they were unloaded and transported to Barnesville over land. Imported glass was ordered in Frederick. Windows bear the names of: Joseph S. Birch, Rev. Gilbert H. McDonald, William Reid, Alousius and Sarah Reid, Lloyd and Ann Jones, Thomas D. Leonard, Sarah Elizabeth Jones, Mrs. C. E. Kingsbury, Zachariah M. Knott, James Ganley. The original oak pews were replaced and the curved colonnades at the altar have been altered. Air conditioning was added along with a sound system.

Mission Priests of St. Mary's:
James Redmond	1814-1816
Michael Carroll	1817-1818
P. J. DeVos	1819-1831
Fr. Jamison	1835
P. Borgnay	1839
M. P. Gallagher	1840-1846
Thomas Foley	1846-1847
F. X. King	1847
J. I. Maguire	1847-1849
Fr. McManus	1850-1851
T. E. Boyle	1852-1853
H. L. Spruyt	1867-1868
J. O. Sullivan	1868-1869

Resident Pastors of St. Mary's:
Joseph S. Birch	1869-1882
Thomas D. Leonard	1882-1888
M. J. Riordan	1888-1899
L. Paul Reynolds	1899-1900
George H. McDonald	1900-1906
George B. Harrington	1906-1920
Michael S. Cuddy	1920-1921

Joseph P. Ritchie   1922-1938
Carl Hess   1938-1942
James Bifield   1942-1946
Phillip Brown   1946-1950
Francis Driscoll   1950-1954
Martin Hyland   1954-1966
George B. Reid   1966-1998
Joseph Kleinstuber   1998

Stations of the Cross [Memorials to or Gifts of:]
I   Jarboe Brosius
II   Charles T. Brosius
III Mercer Jones
IV   W. T. Jones
V   Mr. & Mrs. Jerome Offutt
VI   William & Ann Reid
VII Rev. J. S. Cuddy
VIII St. Mary's Sewing Society
IX   Beulah & Lillian Jones
X   Harry Gormley
XI   Mrs. E. A. Kingsbury
XII Daniel & Margaret Shreve
XIII Mr. & Mrs. J. H.C. Hoyle [to their children]
XIV Mr. & Mrs. J. H. C. Hoyle [by their children]

Archbishop Patrick O'Boyle dedicated the Shrine of Our Lady of Fatima on May 3, 1959. The outdoor shrine is a gift of Bernard Siegel, and on the altar of the indoor shrine is a stone cut from the area where the Blessed Mother appeared to the children in Fatima. The stone was presented by the then-Ambassador of Portugal.

The cemetery behind the church has been in use for over 170 years. The second section was dedicated in 1820 by Father DeVos. Chesapeake and Ohio Canal workers who perished in Cholera epidemics were buried here, as well as parish members.

During the Civil War troops camped in the vicinity of the cemetery and pavilion. Some of the soldiers and officers attended services at St. Mary's during these encampments.

Father Joseph Birch

St. Mary's Roman Catholic Church

10. St. Mary's Rectory

The frame rectory was built in 1867 on lot #23, during the time of Father Spruyt, near the site of the brick rectory. In 1932 the old rectory was demolished and a new brick house was built at a cost of $10,000. This was paid for by Mrs. Winifred Tyson of New York in appreciation of the kindness of Father Birch and Dr. Bowlen. Arthur Hoyle assisted in the construction of the rectory. Fr. Joseph P. Ritchie was pastor at the time. The house is now used for office space and classes. The present rectory is located behind the pavilion. The photograph was taken in 1933.

11. site of Kiernon Manion House

In 1878 Nathan Miles was living in a log house on lot #22. By 1890 Kiernon Manion, Irish immigrant was living here. He was the Justice of the Peace in 1891. His son James was paid for the upkeep of this section of Main Street in 1908-1909. The two-story frame house somewhat resembled the Hilton Cabinet Shop but has been gone for nearly 45 years. It was replaced by the present house built in the 1950's for the Parton sisters. Sydney Earle lives here presently.

12. site of Blacksmith Shop

One of two blacksmith shops in Barnesville, this one was the older of the the two on part of lot #22. It was run by Jacob Stiers, who lived in a house owned by Mary Knott. From 1868 to 1878 Joel H. Wolfe was the blacksmith here. In 1890 Benjamin F. Roberson moved from Greenfield Mills and ran the shop. He remained as the blacksmith here until 1918, when he moved to Dickerson.

13. Zachariah Loy House

Formerly site of the Archie and Claudia Morningstar two-story log house on lot #21. The McLaughlins lived here, and then the Loys. Presently Robert and Donna Mitchell reside here. They had the house raised and expanded the living quarters.

14. site of Solomon Plummer House

There were two houses located on lot #20. John Plummer settled in the fledgling village in 1792. His son Solomon, graduate of the Hays School, lived here in a log house. In 1870 Samuel P. Hays was living in the other house and by 1920 Edgar Morningstar lived there.

15. Barn Hill

This property was purchased as a parcel from the Hays farm by Matilda Rose Duvall during the depression. Mrs. Duvall was an artist of French descent. The French Provincial style house was built from Ace Wrecking Company materials. It has one large front room which served as her studio. The upstairs bedrooms have dormer windows. The outbuildings include a garage and servants quarters. There was also a dirt tennis court. Other occupants include Carlton and Antoinnette Van Emon, Col. and Mrs. Samuel H. Tolbert, who purchased it in 1954, and Mr. and Mrs. Paul Gouillot. Walter and DiAne Fischer purchased the property in 1993 and operated a Bed and Breakfast until 1998.

16. Road to Mouth of Monocacy

The present route of Barnesville Road has been altered from the original "Baltimore Road" which led to the Mouth of Monocacy, through Oakland Mills. There were farms and homesteads along this path, and the road is now bisected by the railroad tracks. One such farm was a 250 acre tract called "Grandmother's Goodwill." The Jeffers family farmed the back section and in 1933 bought the farm. In 1943 they moved into the former Barnesville School after Butke converted it. The Cotters later lived here and Tinker Cotter taught tap dancing in the kitchen on Saturdays. Victor Pepe now owns this farm called "Stella's Delight."

Also along the old road was the home of Nicholas W. and Mary M. Appleby. Parceled from the Fitch farm, it was sold to Daniel Price in 1868. The Applebys were founding members of the Barnesville Methodist Church.

17. The Hays Farm

The original dwelling, built for Leonard I. Hays. The house burned in 1929 and the present frame house was built for tenants in 1933 by Maurice Orme and Clagett C. Hilton. After several additions, the house has eclectic features. The land has remained in the family for over 200 years.

18. Brown's Tenant House

Will and Emily Brown had this house built on a parcel from their farm in 1915 for Will Baker. A two story frame house with center door, and two end chimneys it was later the residence of Charles Fowler.

19. Algie Morningstar House

The original section of this house was built on lot #18 c. 1840 of log. G. Scholls lived here and in 1878 G. S. Nicholls was living here. The frame house was built for Algie Morningstar c. 1911. Frank Fowler has lived here in more recent years. The porch has been enclosed and the exterior was remodeled in 1998.

20. site of Barnesville Methodist Episcopal Church and Cemetery

Built in 1843, this was frame church, on the Montgomery Circuit built to serve the former members of the Bethel Chapel. It was first served by J. M. Jones, followed by Horace Holland. Circuit ledgers for this church include the baptisms of Lindell Virginia Gue and Walker M. Shipley on March 21, 1909 by Rev. Caleb M. Yost, Edna May Morningstar and James Roger Morningstar on November 15, 1938 by Hartwell F. Chandler, and the last listing was Charles Newton Staub on August 27, 1944 by Rev. Morgan.

The cemetery behind
William Alexander of Philadelphia
    Corp Co H. 6th US Cavalry killed 10 Sep 1862
Isaac Bell of New York d 17 Aug 1844 age 35 [mother was a Poole]
Hatton Browne 28 Jan 1801 - 28 Dec 1871
    w Deborah 16 Feb 1866 age 73
James Edelin 27 Mar 1777 - 21 Mar 1852
    w Eleanor 18 Nov 1780 - 28 Sep 1852
Elizabeth Feaster w/o Jacob 3 Jul 1858 age 70
Mr. Griffith of Virginia d. October 1862, CSA
Williminer Harris 22 Jan 1848 age 54
Elizabeth M. Hawkins d 19 Jun 1867 age 22
John H. T. Hays 8 Oct 1813 - 23 Jun 1857
Leonard Hays 30 Jul 1793 - 24 Apr 1864 *
    w Eliza Medora Howard 28 Jun 1807 - 21 Jul 1874
        *stone moved to Monocacy Cemetery, Beallsville
        * 5 Oct 1917
Thomas L. Hays 20 Nov 1816 - 4 Oct 1873
Elisha Howard d 27 Apr 1874 age 84 *
    w Eleanor 12 Jul 1791 - 8 Feb 1873
Dr. Lacy d. 10 Sep 1862 CSA
Hester Ellen McAbee d 17 Jan 1848 age 18 w/o John T.
Jacob Nichols 2 Oct 1788 - 25 Nov 1857
    w Sarah 19 Feb 1798 - 25 Nov 1867
Colmore Offutt 7 Feb 1855 age 54
    w Mary Anne 6 Feb 1788 - 2 Sep 1845
Mary Plummer 4 May 1817 - 18 Jun 1874
Philemon N. Plummer 16 Dec 1815 - 26 Oct 1861
    w Sarah A. 20 Sep 1820 - 26 Feb 1873

Sarah A. Plummer d 19 Jul 1866 age 35
Laura V. Pyles w/o Richard T. 6 Nov 1842 - 17 Sep 1865
John Smith 18 Dec 1801 - 19 Jul 1872
Abigail Trail 5 Jun 1789 - 10 May 1857 w/o William
James P. Wade 7 Aug 1825 - 15 Apr 1858   * 2 Sep 1937
    w Harriet Ann 16 Feb 1828 - 26 Jan 1906   * 2 Sep 1937
    d Mary Elizabeth 1 Jun 1853 - 23 Feb 1937   * 2 Sep 1937
    d Alice 10 Dec 1855 - 30 Oct 1889   * 2 Sep 1937
    s James Perry, Jr. d. 31 Aug 1858 age 1-2-10 * 2 Sep 1937
Sarah Ellen Nichols White d 15 May 1856 age 26-1-19
    w/o Benjamin Stephen d/o Jacob N. & Sarah E. Nichols *
    d Sarah Ellen 0-3-21 * 10 Oct 1921 moved to Monocacy

Mrs. L. Anderson lived in a house next to the church in 1878, but the house is no longer standing.

21. site of Roberson-Ryman House

In 1878 Mrs. Wilhelmina Sherman lived in a house on lot #16. In 1890 Benjamin F. Roberson, blacksmith, moved here from Greenfield. He moved to Dickerson in 1918, selling the house to Homer Ryman, mail carrier. The house was burned for a fire drill in the 1960's, then Ernest L. Butt built his brick house on the lot.

22. site of Grange Hall

This building was a two-story structure, located across from the entrance to St. Mary's Pavilion on a parcel of lot #16. A rectangular building, of frame construction, it had two front doors, a center chimney and two windows in the front, sides and in the back. The downstairs had two rooms, and upstairs was the meeting hall. Elections were held here when the building was still in use. The Grange was incorporated on January 6, 1883 with the following members: Benjamin F. White, George R. Hays, Isaac Young, Leonard I. Hays, John W. Brown, Frederick P. Hays, John A. Jones, William C. Brown, Leonidas Jones, John S. Gott, Abraham G. Harris, Isaac T. Jones, and Edward J. Chiswell. The five dincters that were elected to manage the corporation were: Edward I. Chiswell, Benjamin F. White, George R. Hays, Isaac Young, and Leonard I. Hays.

23. Hays Family Cemetery

Leonard Hays d 14 Sep 1822 age 63
    w Eleanor 25 Oct 1833 age 73
    d Elizabeth w/o John A. Trundle 22 Feb 1818 - 30 Jan 1855
Samuel S. Hayes 2 Apr 1787 - 5 Sep 1857
    w Anna 7 Sep 1796 - 8 Mar 1855
    d Sarah 28 Dec 1823 - 17 Jan 1847
    d Martha M. Hayes Nichols d 1 Sep 1840 age 17

24. John Brown Farm

In Nathan Thomas Veatch's original 1812 town plan, West Harris Road was called Church Street, and the John Brown House was on the corner of Church Street and Main Street on lot #15. The house was L-shaped and was of the Victorian style, with a vine covered porch, ornately decorated with gingerbread trim. The side porch lead to the kitchen. The picket fence and the archway were covered with Dorothy Perkins roses. In 1860 Hatton Brown, shoemaker, was living here. Don Benson built the current house.

25. William Brown House

Built c. 1900 this house is a Federal style with hipped roof and dormers. It was built for William C. Brown, on land parceled from the John Brown farm. Presently James and Mildred Callear live here. The cover photograph was taken of the barn on the property.

26. Daybreak Farm

In 1796 Joseph Harris owned over 1,100 acres of property which stretched from Barnesville to the foot of Sugarloaf Mountain. He had tenants and family members living in various locations on the land. Included was Bethel Chapel, a Methodist Episcopal log church which Harris stipulated in his will to remain open to all members to use as a place of worship. When he died in 1797 the property was divided into seven lots. Mary Harris inherited part of the land which was divided again after her death. The old house was abandoned; and a new one was built in 1850 where Joseph H. C. Hoyle was living with his family during the Civil War. Confederate Soldiers stayed here for a week while practicing drills and maneuvers. The Yankees, not wanting to harm any civilians, asked the Hoyles to go upstairs in their house and stay while they drove the Rebs out. On top of the hill near Harris Road cannon were set up facing the mountain. There was no fighting, but it was a tale the Hoyle children often re-told in later years. In 1907 the community raised the red barn. Joseph H. C. Hoyle conveyed the land to Elmer Hoyle in 1918. In 1939 Elmer Hoyle sold to W. Marshall and Eleanor White for $5,000. Mr. White had a new well dug, added a kitchen, bathroom, and a storage area. In 1964 White split up the acreage, selling 32 acres to Sharon Farr, Mr. and Mrs. Robert Chapman purchased the house, barn and 44 acres, and the old house and 52 acres were sold to E. F. Cox. J. Edward Day, former Postmaster General gave the farm it's name, Daybreak, after he purchased the property in the 1960's.

27. site of Hays School

A one room school, built c. 1819, was situated just to the right of the John W. Brown farm house. It measured 60' X 30' and could accommodate 100 children. The desks had drawers and a shelf was around the inner wall for lunch pails, with pegs under the shelf for wraps. Two tin-plate wood burning stoves heated the school and the teacher's desk was at the front. Thomas Carr Lannan, graduate of Belfast College, Ireland was the principal here from 1830-36. Mr. Rogers and Mr. McGary assisted him at some point, while they were candidates for holy orders in the Catholic Church. Some of the students who attended were:

Hamilton Anderson 1830-36
Thomas Austin 1830-36
Lemuel L. Beall 1824-30
Avery Bell 1830-36
Richard Belt 1830-36
Gassaway Grimes 1830-36
Edward Hays 1827-33
Martha Hays 1832-1838
Sarah Ellen Hays 1828-1834
Henrietta Harwood 1830-36
Christian Hershey 1832-1838
David Hershey 1828-34
John Hershey 1830-36
King Jay 1830-36
Stephen Jay 1830-36
Thomas Johnson 1830-32
Ellen Jones 1830-36

Caroline Murphy 1839-45
Mary Nichols 1832-38
Thomas Nichols 1830-36
Catherine Pearre 1837-42
George Pearre 1829-1835
James Pearre 1833-1839
Mary Pearre 1835-1841
William Pearre 1834-1840
Mary Plummer 1830-36
Philemon Plummer 1830-36
John Poole Sellman 1850-56
William O. Sellman 1824-1830
Richard Thompson 1835-1841
Frances Trail 1830-36
Jane Trail 1830-36
Mortimer Trail 1830-6
Oscar Trail 1830-36

28. John W. Brown Farm

John W. Brown built the original part of this house c. 1870. The center gable, five bay section was added c. 1900 by Hatton Darby Brown. The house is two and a half stories with center foyer, two front living rooms, dining room large kitchen and summer kitchen in back. The L-shaped porch is trimmed with gingerbread work. The back of the house has a two story porch. Electricity and plumbing were installed about 1936. In the early 1960's a parcel was sold to Robert Pumphrey who raised and trained Tennessee Walking horses. In 1981 Richard Poole Brown sold the farm to William and Jacquelin Sheehan.

29. Bowlen-Kessler House

This house was built on lot #14 in the 1870's by Nathan Talbott for Dr. George W. and Mary McFarland Bowlen. The Clements lived there, and later sold it to Herbert and Mary Kessler. It was conveyed to the Knott's and then Leonard Offutt. It was built in the Federal Style, with a metal hipped roof and center chimney. The addition was completed in the 1940's. Clifton and Doris Hill are the current owners.

30. Clarence Colemar Offutt House

In the original town plot this was lot 13 and John Plummer owned the property in 1820. In 1878 it was owned by Nathan Talbott who added to the original log house which dates to 1790. Each of the three sections has a separate stone cellar. The present house is Federal style, with four over four, double hung windows, and patches in the floor show where a stairwell had previously been. The beams are all numbered and lettered as though they were moved here and re-assembled. The house was renovated in the 1940's at which time the porch was removed. Tom and Susan Pignone purchased the house in 1971.

31. Mary Morningstar House

Leonard Hays, Sr. had a log cabin on what became lot #12 by 1743. The frame house was built by William T. Hilton in 1824. The 1860 census and 1878 map show Thomas Pyles here. In 1888 Richard T. Pyles lived here. In the 1930's Burt and Carrie Nicholson operated a store and lived here. Mary Morningstar purchased the house during the depression. The log section is two-story and has two rooms on each floor. The doors to the bedrooms have the original H hinges, and all the doors are of Georgia pine. The 19th century addition by Hilton is separated from the log section by a center hallway with a graceful stairway leading to the second floor. There are three attics at various levels with separate accesses. One may have been a bedroom for hired hands. The house is situated on three acres of land. The two-story porch with ornately carved columns supporting the latticework second story is trimmed with gingerbread bric-a-brac. The house was remodeled by David Johnson in 1997.

32. Jerome Offutt House

Gabriel Wothen had a cabin on lot #11 by 1820. In 1850 Isaac Pyles was living here followed in 1880 by Rebecca Pyles. The present house was built in 1914 for Charles Brosius. It is a Colonial Revival with a hipped roof, three bays and a dormer. An addition was made during a renovation. Later Mary Loretta and Jerome Offutt lived here, and their son Leonard raised mink commercially on the property. The house has a foyer leading to a dining room which has curved plaster walls, four bedrooms, back porch and a lovely view of Sugarloaf Mountain from the back. There was another home between this house and the next one owned by James F. and Fanny Fitch in 1870, and then Anne C. Orme in 1880.

33. Hersberger House

This house is on land which was originally Jeremiah Hays's inheritance of 184 acres in 1783. The property contained three small log houses and a barn at that time and was listed as "Jeremiah's Park." The property was left to Abraham by his father, Leonard Hays. The present house was built on lot #10 of logs for Abraham Hays c. 1820 and later stuccoed. It was built on a fieldstone foundation, reinforced by poured concrete. It has a single run open-string staircase, with central hallway flanked by two rooms on each side. Hays sold this lot in 1832 to Jacob Nicholls for $225.00. Jacob Nicholls lived in the house until he died in 1869, when it passed to his daughter Harriet A. Wade. Mrs. Wade sold the house to Mary E. White in 1883. Dr. Joseph N. White ran his maternity hospital here beginning in 1912. The glassed in upstairs porch that was used for new mothers to enjoy fresh air and sunshine has been removed. There were five rooms available along the main hall. He sold the property to Arthur C. Hersberger in 1923. Later, this was the home of Mr. and Mrs. John Sears c. 1976. The current owners are Tim Fitch and Joel Slackman.

34. Old Barnesville Store

On a parcel of lot #10 the old Barnesville store supplied everything from Queensware to dry goods. Richard P. Hays was one of the merchants who ran the old store. John Hilton is listed in the 1860 census as the merchant. Another storekeeper was Luther Cecil according to the 1870 census.

35. Stonestreet-Gittings House

The present property was formerly lot #9 with two log houses. One was owned by Abigail Hays Trail who sold to William E. Murphy. Another house on the property was occupied by Sarah Pormellon in 1820, Elias Moulden, carpenter, and his wife Mary from 1850 to 1872, and then Charles T. and Mary F. Smith. The present house was built in 1861 by Leonard Hays, Sr. for Richard P. Hays whose wife Bettie sold it on the two acre lot to Priscilla J. Poole in 1896 who then sold to Dr. Joseph Harris Stonestreet of Charles County, and it has remained in the family since 1899. Gertrude Wood, daughter of R. Vinton Wood, married Dr. Stonestreet and had the grillwork added to the house. On October 17, 1931 the lawn of the Stonestreet House was the scene of the wedding of Virginia Worthington Stonestreet to Edward Francis Gittings. The family silver and instruments used by Dr. Stonestreet are still in the family. The house is Federal style with Victorian details, a two story brick structure with a hipped roof. A frame, two story addition is in the rear of the house. Robert Stonestreet lives here presently.

36. Luther Cecil House

This part of lot #9 was unimproved in 1820. Luther Cecil moved to Barnesville in 1869, from Comus, when he married Mary C. Hawkins. He raised his family here, all contributors to the town thriving economy. While Daisy Cecil was teaching at Barnesville School, she boarded here with her uncle and family. In various census records he is listed as the store keeper, hotel keeper, mail carrier and his son Murrell, later owner, was a well driller. The other son ran the store after Luther retired. Daughter Clara, known as Callie, taught at Barnesville School. James Robert Lillard and wife Stella bought the house in 1925, moving from Sellman. Their son James Robert, Jr., and his wife Marjorie have made this their lifetime home.

37. Lillard's Garage

Built in 1940 to house the trucks for Mr. Lillard's business, this is the site where Barnesville citizens currently cast their election ballots in the Capitol Perfection cigar box.

Ballot Box — A Barnesville voter selects three candidates for the town commission before placing his ballot in a cigar box. For the story on municipal elections in six towns, see

Sentinel Photo by Paul C. Haller

38. Pyles Store

The General Store carried a wide variety of products, and also Esso gasoline. Men sat on the bench in front of the store and the women of Barnesville said the men couldn't come home and eat supper until they'd sat there and talked. The post office was also located here until 1951. Mr. Robert Lillard ran the store in 1920's-1940's and later leased it to Thomas W. Brown, and then John and Larry Anderson. Mr. and Mrs. Beverly Thomas were the last merchants to run the store. It closed in 1968 and currently houses a gift shop. The Thomas's supplied oranges and candy for the annual Santa visit before Christmas. Pictured below are Maurice Ricketts and Bub Brown.

39. Charles T. Dixon House

The log house of Mrs. Sarah Hilton Claggett on lot #8 was replaced by this two story frame house after 1895. After Charles Dixon conveyed the house to Eberly Dixon, Clark and Bonnie Brown purchased the house. Several additions and alterations have been made to the original seven room house, including a family room, enlarged kitchen and an additional bedroom.

40. Boswell House

In 1820, lot #7 was unimproved. Carpenter Nathan Talbott owned this lot in 1879. An old log house preceded the frame house built in 1912 for Oscar Thomas Cecil. In 1922 Mr. Cecil died suddenly and the family moved to Baltimore. Mr. and Mrs. Shannon sold to Albert Easter, whose wife built the garage. Connie Wrede lived here prior to Peter Menke who added more rooms to the rear of the house after he purchased it.

41. Francis Knott House

Parceled from lot #7, Francis and Mary Jane Cecil Knott lived here after the Civil War. The Jordans lived here in the late 1930's and had an extensive annual Christmas display. Wilson Jordan had been a preacher in Clarksburg prior to moving to Sellman and then Barnesville, where he was an electrician. Garrett Cooley lived here and then this house served as the parsonage for the Baptist Church from approximately 1940-1970. A list of pastors who lived here is on page 87. G. T. Merrel was living here in 1976. Presently the home of Alan Perlmeter.

42. Community Hall

Originally lot #6, this was the site of the Thomas Vetach house in 1820. The Town Hall was built in 1922 with funds raised by the citizens of Barnesville. A corporation was formed August 7, 1925 with the following as Trustees: Clagett C. Hilton, J. Forrest Gott, F. Leonard Hays, Milton Phillips and Arthur C. Hersberger. It is of white clapboard construction and rectangular in shape with three windows down each side, and two in the front. There was a stage inside, but the interior was remodeled for a residence. It was sold to Monocacy Lions Club in 1947 and in 1953 the club sold it to Mrs. Mildred Shoup. Because the land won't percolate the future of this building is uncertain.

43. Dr. Garrett Cooley House

The devoted, self-taught, veterinarian who was always "on-call" lived in this house which was built c. 1941. Dr. Charles Garrett Cooley raised chickens out back, which he sold. When George and Georgiana Wood purchased the home, they converted the chicken houses into an antique furniture and gift shop.

Leonard Street's colorful nickname "Stove Street" was coined from the stove pipes coming out of the windows of the shanties. The occupants could not afford to build chimneys. Only three of these houses remain from the original black settlement.

44. Harold F. Cooley House

This house was built c. 1949 for Harold Franklin Cooley. It replaced an earlier house on this lot. Each summer before the Barnesville picnic, Mr. Cooley would manicure the shoulders of the roads leading into Barnesville. Mrs. Nellie Cooley still resides in the home.

45. Clarence Brown House

This is one of the original houses of Stove Street, built c. 1876 by Nathan Talbott. It has two rooms on each floor with a center hall. The house was sold to the Poole family, and then to Major and Mrs. Howard Warren. In the 1980's William Price and Cherry Barr purchased the house as a rental property. It has been remodeled and a kitchen and bath were added. Pat Jeffrey purchased the house in recent years. A similar house was next to this one, also built by Nathan Talbott. It was the home of Charles Brown.

46. Charles C. Claggett

Charles Claggett built this house on his 11 acre farm c. 1880. The house was left to his daughter Bessie, who lived to be 104 years old. The house sat abandoned for several years before Mark and Julia Torrey bought and restored the house. Mark found a violin in the attic, made in Germany in the 1800's which he also had restored. There were two more houses like this, the Thomas Piles House where Charles Spencer later lived, and the George Claggett house, which is only slightly visible in the winter when the hedge is bare.

47. Garver-Menke House

Built for Mrs. Nellie Garver in 1935, this Cape Cod style frame house features nine dormers and a screened in porch. The two-story house has five bedrooms, a full basement and still has its original furnace. In 1950 the house was sold to George and Dorothy Menke who lived there until 1974. The current owners, John and Meg Menke operate an astronomy observatory manufacturing business and have customers worldwide. John was a founding member of the Sugarloaf Citizens Association in 1972, and served on the Montgomery County Council from 1974-1978.

48. site of Ward's Mill

Thomas Ward's Mill was a grist mill near the Little Monocacy which once had a high water table—enough for vessels to navigate. It was in operation prior to the turn of the century, but the water power diminished, and grain was no longer ground in mills after the 1930's. The house is closer to the road than the mill was. The house is currently owned by Charles and Mary Lou Anderson Jones. Charles feels at home here since his ancestors once lived here.

49. Henry Ambush House

This house dates to 1895. It is a two story frame house of three bays with a center door and end chimney. The one story front porch accentuates the pitch of the hillside into which this house is built. Henry and Martha Ambush were the last occupants of this house.

50. Barnesville Public School

   The Board of Education purchased this 3/4 acre portion of lot #5 from Frederick and Ida L. Hays for $50.00 in 1896. In 1820 the cabin of Abraham Hays occupied this site, but in 1896 a two room school was built here at a cost of $750.00. It was furnished for $60.00. The school had a coal stove to heat the building. The coal supply was stored in the basement, or under the front porch. John "Chalk" Johnson was responsible for getting the stove going each morning. There were two privies out back, and a water pump in front. The teacher rang a hand bell each morning and then opened with prayer, salute to the flag and a song. Grades one through six were in one room, seven and eight in the other, with a slate blackboard across the front of both rooms. There was a 15 minute recess in the mid-morning and mid afternoon, with an hour break for lunch. School began at 9:00 AM and lasted until 3:30 PM. The average attendance was 35-40. In the front vestibule was a place to hang wraps, a basin to wash up, and a water pitcher. The following year $10.00 worth of books were purchased as a library for the school. The first teachers were C. M. Burdette who taught until 1902 and Maisey Brown. The community requested an addition for the school at this time.

   On October 28, 1902 this item appeared in the Sentinel: "The event of the day at Barnesville on Friday last was the entertainment given by the public school in honor of Columbus Day. At an early hour the people began gathering from all quarters and the Grange Hall was packed to the utmost, with quite enough outside to fill it again, and many having to return home without getting near the door...The movements of the different classes and pupils were like clockwork, no bell being used, and showed a high order of discipline. At this we are not surprised, as the teacher, Miss Margie Hargett, is said to be one of the best disciplinarians in the state. Prof. Story presided at the organ with his usual grace and skill and added much to the interest of the occasion."

   In 1905 the school board voted to defer the addition for the school and in 1906 H. Ceadell was one of the teachers. In 1912 the community requested High School curriculum classes to be taught in Barnesville. In 1916 Miss Clara "Callie" Cecil was the teacher for several years. Electric lighting was installed in 1926.

   Mary Morningstar recalls attending classes here from the first grade until the fourth grade when her family moved to Gaithersburg. Her teacher was Miss Daisy Cecil. Some of the other teachers remembered by Barnesville residents include: Eloise Renshaw, who boarded at the Hays house; followed by Courtney Burdette Wade from Hyattstown, Eleanor Ray, who boarded at the Sellman house with Lucy Fitzsimmons, Ethel Luhn, Elsie Warfel, Hazel Horton, and Miss Young, who taught here in 1930's.

Miss Meany was the supervisor and would come in to test students occasionally. She was in charge of the Clarksburg, Comus, Hyattstown, and Barnesville schools. After 1933, students attended classes in Poolesville. The building was sold to Arthur and Helen Bready in 1940, who sold it to William and Loretta Butke. They began remodeling the school, and sold it in 1943 to the Jeffers who completed the renovation into a private residence. Part of the old blackboard was used to make hearth. Mrs. Julia Jeffers was the town clerk from 1953 until 1993. The home is currently owned by Paul R. Stevens.

51. Baptist Church

The cornerstone was laid in 1869 and the original building was of log construction. Later clapboard siding was added to the rectangular building, with gable front facade, bell tower, white weatherboard exterior. Example of mid-nineteenth century rural church architecture. The congregation was officially organized on September 24, 1871 as a result of the missionary labors of Joseph H. Jones. Barnesville Church was his "Monument" and the following signed the Covenant and became charter members:

Joseph H. Jones
Leah Criswell
Charles R. Darby
Mary J. Darby
Samuel Darby
William W. Darby
E. D. Griffith
F. M. Griffith
Jemima A. Griffith
Prudence Griffith
Laura Gott

Richard T. White
Sarah Harris
F. R. Hilton
William T. Hilton
Lizzie Jones
Rachel Oden
Ann P. Sellman
William O. Sellman
Mary E. White
Joel Hamilton Wolfe
Anna Mary Linthicum Wolfe

Elected at that meeting were:

Rev. Joseph Hawkins Jones, Pastor
Richard T. White, Deacon
William O. Sellman, Assistant Deacon
Samuel Darby, Clerk

In 1954 sufficient money was in the building fund to add the Sunday School rooms and to enlarge the sanctuary. In 1971 a new parsonage was built on Peach Tree Road, which was sold in 1972. The current parsonage was purchased that year. In 1982 the entire church was refurbished, to include new carpet and pews and exterior siding.

Pastors of the Church:

Joseph H. Jones	1871
William M. Davis	1872
John W. Marsh	1873-1874
Hilleary E. Hatcher	1878-1886
James H. Wright	1887
L. R. Millburn	1891-1892
S. R. White	1893-1899
Lewis Jones	1900
J. L. Lodge	1901
R. S. Owens	1902
R. A. Smith	1904
F. B. Cowell	1909-1911
J. C. McFadden	
E. C. Burke	1916
P. Rowland Wagner	1917
S. A. Shaver	1926-1928
James M. Coleman	1928
H. H. Nicoll	1929-1931
H. M. Hall	1931-1933
H. Marvin Flinn	1933-1936
Herbert Cooper	1937
Thomas Fleming	1947-1949
William F. Shoup	1950-1952
Horace C. DuBois	1953-1969
Jeddie DeFries	1969-1994
Jim Painter	1994-1995
Blaine Welker	1995-

H. Mortimer Hilton began the Sunday School with a class of three boys, and lived to see it flourish with 75 scholars before he passed away. The Superintendent was E. T. Dixon. The Women's Missionary Society was formed in 1933 and has sent supplies to frontier Indian pastors, as well as to China and other foreign fields. In the 1950's and 60's Edith DuBois served as organist and directed the choir. She was followed by Lorraine DeFries.

52. George Tyler Funk Farm

"Clean Drinking" and "Mount Vale" were owned by John Poole who died in 1814. His children were unable to divide the property equably, and in 1835 had the courts divide his holdings. This section, parcel #2 of 332 acres went to Eliza Poole Hays and her husband, Leonard. The house was built prior to 1865, probably for one of their children. Leonard Hays died in 1864, leaving this property to son Frederick Pocreus Hays, along with one horse, one feather bed, bedstead, furniture, gold watch and $500. The house overlooked the Baltimore Road, an important main artery. He married Ida Hempstead in 1881. In 1917 the stones from the Sellman-Poole Family Cemetery were moved to Monocacy Cemetery in Beallsville. In 1919 Harry Savage bought the farm from Hays. In 1929 Savage defaulted on his mortgage, and the farm was advertised "Bordering on the concrete State Highway, fine mansion house containing 12 rooms, large porches, and cellar, two bank barns, corn house, wagon shed, ice house, dairy house, 90 foot chicken house, meat house, blacksmith shop and tenant house." The house was constructed in three sections, but the rear ell was removed. The English basement was under back section of the house. In 1943 Hatton and Richard P. Brown purchased the farm, and leased it to Carson Ward 1952-1962. In 1965 the Browns sold it to Mrs. Garvin Tankersley and it served for a while as the Conoy Club House. The land has been divided and part is now the Conoy development.

53. Sellman House

This house may have been built prior to 1783, when one shows up on tax records for this property. At that time Frederick Sprigg owned 1,170 acres with an old frame house, log kitchen, corn and meat house, two old frame tobacco houses with four tenement houses. It has a stone chimney with a double fireplace, pothooks for kettles, and original fireplaces in the other rooms. The entire west end of the house was log, now covered by clapboards. The east end of the house was added later, incorporating the stairs to the second floor between the two sections. Daughter Priscilla married John Poole and inherited part of this farm, and they spent their lives here. He established a tannery here which was later run by Ira W. Elder. In 1810 Poole also acquired five lots in Barnesville and an additional 600 acres. When he died in 1829 the acreage was divided among his children. Ann Priscilla married William Oliver Sellman, and inherited lot #1. William O. Sellman died in 1884 and his estate was divided into several tracts; the part which included the house was purchased by Mrs. Sellman and two daughters. It was conveyed to Richard Sellman in 1918, who stipulated that it go to Charles B. Sellman who sold it to Beverly and Sallie Thomas in 1947. They operated the Barnesville Store until 1968.

54. Lawrence Hilton Price House

Built in 1917 for Deborah Jane Burdette and Lawrence Hilton Price, this Colonial Revival style house with hipped roof has a rear addition and sunroom added on the west side. The front porch is original to the house and has an excellent view of Sugarloaf Mountain. There are two staircases. Previously there was a gasoline powered engine which pumped water to a tank in the attic to supply the house with water. It sold to Brad and Glenda Crowley in 1970.

55. Thomas Story House

Built c. 1869 by Nathan Talbott for Prof. Thomas Story who was born in Hancock. Story was later clerk in the U. S. Treasury Department, and came to Barnesville in 1869, where he taught school for 19 years, composed music, played the organ, and the lyrics to his song "The Bold Monocacy" which are included below. It was written while he was waiting for the swollen river to return to it's banks, and he could return to his sweetheart, Sedonia Hilton, in Barnesville.

Edward Story, son of Thomas, is listed in the 1910 census as a professional baseball player, perhaps it was he that commissioners attempted to bar from street games! He later became a bank teller in Poolesville, and audited the books for Barnesville, and also was a Notary Public. Later, Carson Ward lived here, but Robert Ruhl and Claire O'Meara live here presently.

THE BANKS OF THE BOLD MONOCACY

I have roamed far away about the land I have sailed far, far across the sea;
I have left behind Old Maryland and the Banks of the bold Monocacy.
And there in a cottage by the hill, I have left one who's all the world to me;
But I know that she loves and trusts me still on the Banks of the Bold Monocacy.

Chorus:
O soon I'll cross the raging main, my Maryland I soon again shall see,
And soon I'll greet my love again on the banks of the Bold Monocacy.

How sad and how heavy was my heart and how fondly my darling clung to me
When I from her was forced to part by the banks of the Bold Monocacy.
I tenderly kissed the tears away that down her cheeks were flowing free,
And I told here I'd soon come back to stay on the Banks of the Bold Monocacy.

Chorus

I have longed for many a weary day for the time to come when I'd be free,
To take my journey and away to the Banks of the Bold Monocacy.
Sweet visions of my every slumbering fill of the dear one I'm longing to see,
Of the dear little cottage by the hill, on the Banks of the Bold Monocacy.

Chorus

Oh now how with joy my heart does bound as I think what a happy hour twill be,
When I shall hear this well known sound the rippling of the Bold Monocacy
And dearer to me than all the rest I will greet my darling true to me,
And I'll fold her forever to my breast on the Banks of the Bold Monocacy.

56. Thomas O. White House

This house was the last to be built by William Thomas Hilton. Constructed in 1904, just four years before his death, it features beautiful Victorian Paladin windows, Federal-style garlands, Georgian-style window over the front door, archways with Doric columns between the rooms, beveled glass mirrors over the mantels, and carved chestnut trim. The formal alcove in the entry hall is an elegant place to receive guests. The music and dining rooms have natural chestnut paneling. The house sits on a blue stone base, of stone quarried in Frederick County. Thomas O. White and family lived here until 1938 when Laura White sold to William and Mary Lankford, who sold to Spencer James and Frances Fisher. The Fishers raised 56 foster children during the years they occupied the house. It later was purchased by Paul and Trudy Meissner.

Built on the site of Thomas Hilliard's cabin, this was lot #4 prior to 1820. George Reid had sold the lot to Nathan Talbott in 1870 and the Talbott Hotel was constructed in 1876. The hotel was destroyed on March 28, 1894 in a fire. After the death of Nathan Talbott, the property was auctioned in 1902. At that time it still had a carriage house, three out buildings, stable, well and well house, and a barn.

57. Harold Bryan Barr House

In 1900 Robert F. Wyatt operated a grocery store in part of this house, and lived with his family in the other section. Later, Virgie Jameson conveyed this house to Estelle, who married Harold Bryan Barr. In the early 1930's, the Barrs operated a store in part of the house which had a separate entrance on the south side. Donald Barr, their son, and his wife Mary presently reside in the home.

58. Arthur Hallman House

Arthur and Cora Hallman built this house in the 1920's. Mr. Norris is living here currently.

59. Hilton's Funeral Home

Allen S. Orme is shown living here in 1879. He was and undertaker and wheelwright. Elias Moulden and John Coughlin worked for him. As an offshoot from the carpentry business, William T. Hilton began building caskets in the 1860's. Caskets were lined with fabric interiors, made by his wife Sarah. When Clagett Hilton took over the business, his wife Alonnie assisted with the liners. Clagett Hilton built the horse drawn hearse in 1903 to transport coffins from home parlors to the gravesite. In 1910 he purchased a motorized hearse. The house was purchased in 1930 by William B. Hilton. The Hilton Funeral Home has been located here for 65 years and caskets are now purchased already constructed.

William T. Hilton　　　　**Clagett C. Hilton**

1903 Hearse

Funeral Home in 1933

60. site of Barnesville Academy

The Hays School had served area students since 1819. When the Barnesville Academy was built in 1860, J. Benjamin Hodges was the teacher and this was a "pay-school." Tuition was one dollar per student per quarter. During the Civil War the school sustained damage when the Army camped around the grounds and used property for fuel. In the 1865 listing of county schools, Barnesville is recorded as school #7 district 3, on the hill opposite the Episcopal Church. In 1868-9 there were 66 students, and the teacher was Henry C. Hickerson. Professor Thomas Story began his 19 year tenure in the fall of 1869. In 1871 the school burned, and a place to hold classes had to be rented. The board ordered a new school to be built and on March 17, 1874. The contract was awarded to Nathan T. Talbott. The new building was 24 X 26 with a vestibule and furnished with Soper's patent desks. Repairs were made in 1887 at a cost of $40.00. In 1880 the teacher was V. D. Shaw. Again in 1889 repairs were made at a cost of $40.00. For two weeks in mid-February 1890 the school was closed while Prof. Thomas Story was ill. Claggett Hilton was among those who attended this school. New furniture was purchased in 1893 costing $55.00. In 1895 $300.00 was spent rebuilding the old school with an additional $40.00 for furniture. The school closed in 1896 when the new school opened. A 1930 deed states that William B. Hilton purchased this property, the old school was torn down in 1929 and the William B. Hilton house was built c. 1931. Both Hilton homes are presently located on this property.

61. Carl Burner house

Mac Bruner built this house for his niece Mary Butler, and her husband Carl Burner. The lumber for this house came from the Butler farm near White's Ferry in 1933. James and Jane Parsley lived here from 1976-1992. Laura Kittleman and Tom Yeatts live here now.

62. Paul Ehrlich House

Built by Mac Bruner for his daughter Mary and her husband Bryan Phillips c. 1915. The wood for the house was brought from Bruner's sister's farm at White's Ferry. Half of the porch was enclosed later, when Mr. Phillips was convalescing. In the late 1930's to 40's the Elkins and Mrs. Mary E. Dudley lived here. The Ehrlichs added a room on the first floor and enclosed the rest of the porch. Later, a second story was added to the addition. Woody Bailey is living here at the present time.

63. Oscar K. Poole House

This house was ordered from Sears Roebuck and assembled by Oscar K. Poole. It is a Colonial Revival with hipped roof, and dormers. The house has stucco siding and the interior woodwork is mostly oak and chestnut. The coal furnace with centrally located register in the hallway has been replaced with modern central heat and air conditioning. Milton and Algie Phillips lived here followed by Elmer Painter and Mae Hildebrand. Currently William Price and Cherry Barr are the owners, and have converted the garage into their office.

64. J. Forrest Gott House

Parceled from the Fink farm, Oscar K. Poole built this house in 1912 for J. Forest and Ethel Wood Gott. Albert Dawson Wotton purchased the home in 1957 and lived here until the house sold to Pat and Peg Pateros who later sold to George K. Miller in 1983.

65. Frederick Hays House

Oscar K. Poole built this frame house in 1919 for Frederick and Ida Lee Hempstead Hays. It was ordered from Sears Roebuck, and arrived via rail. They moved here from the "Mount Vale" farm property. William Myers added a swimming pool in 1970, Eugene Kacacharow now resides here.

66. Thomas G. Mossburg House

Built c. 1909 by Oscar K. Poole for Thomas G. Mossburg who lived here until the mid-1940's. Later Dr. Yohn lived here followed by Dr. Gordon M. Smith in the 1960's. Michael Finn was living here in the 1980s. Glen and Susan Pearcy live here presently.

67. White-Fink Farm

William B. White owned a large tract of the land called "Prospect Hill." Many of the homes along this stretch were parceled off of this property. Later Walter Fink purchased the farm and one of his heirs resides on part of the land. Scott Meissner now lives here.

68. Brewer House

Built for Ed Darby in 1918, Newton and Ruth Chiswell Brewer purchased the house and lived here subsequently. The current owners, Dalis Davidson and Houston Miller grow herbs and raise sheep here to supply wool for the yarn shop. She cleans, cards, spins and knits it for her customers.

69. Judge Noyes House

Built for Reginald and Mary Hays Darby c. 1900, this property was known as "Briarfield." Other owners include Carl Von Dem Busche, Lowell B. Moon and Judge Alfred Duncan Noyes. The exterior appearance of the house remains much the same today as it did nearly a century ago.

70. Christ Episcopal Church

Early settlers of the area attended Monocacy Chapel in Beallsville until St. Peter's was constructed in Poolesville. The members who lived in Barnesville then petitioned for their own chapel, which was constructed on land donated in 1872 by Mrs. Eliza Hays and her daughter. The builder was William T. Hilton, who utilized a mid-Victorian style plan. The church was consecrated December 19, 1878 by the Right Rev. William Pinckney, D. D., L. L. D. Assistant Bishop of Maryland officiating, assisted by seven rectors. The stained glass altar windows were donated by the Belt and Hays families. St. Peter's Church in Poolesville was the parent church, and its' pastors served Barnesville until the mid-1940's. Lawrence H. Price, Jr. and Elizabeth Hays were the last two members to be confirmed here. The building was then converted to Hilton's Shop and the sign currently over the door previously hung at the Hilton Woodworking Mill in Barnesville. The original plaster inside has deteriorated and the use of the building as a workshop has obscured the features of the church. It sits on approximately five acres of land.

Pastors who served Christ Chapel

Rev. Henry Thomas	1878-1888
Rev. W. P. Griggs	1890-1911
Rev. William R. Bushby	1912-1912
Rev. C. D. Lafferty	1913-1915
Rev. A. J. Smith	1915-1918
Rev. E. P. Wroth	1920-1922
Rev. B. Griffiths	1923-1926
Rev. George C. Shears	1927-1928
Rev. Guy H. Crook	1929-1942

71. Barnesville Post Office

On October 5, 1990 the post office was moved to its current location, renting space from Hilton's carpet store. There are 330 box holders with 35 deliveries. Maureen Webster is the current Postmaster. When retired Postmaster Ida Lu Brown was commissioned in 1951, postage was three cents an ounce. The postmaster's annual salary was $1,914.88, based on stamp sales. The 38 post office boxes were rented for ten cents a quarter, although the fee was usually borne by the postmaster when customers forgot to pay it.

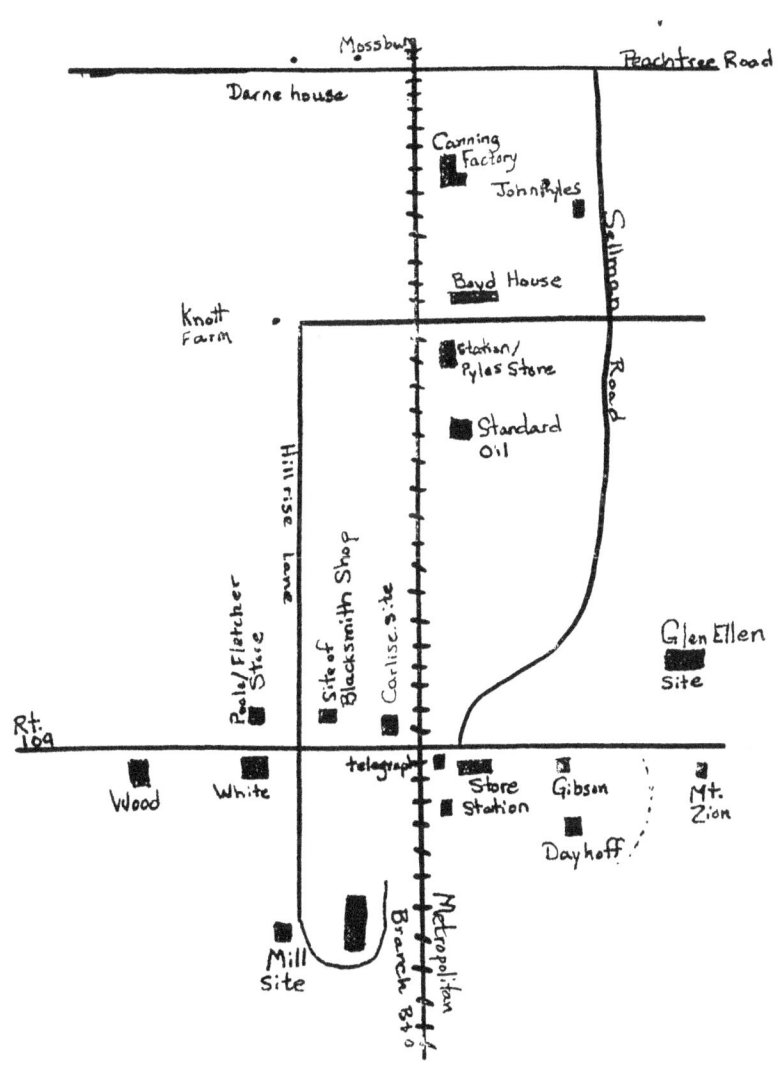

MAP OF SELLMAN

CHAPTER THREE
SELLMAN

Postmasters

William O. Sellman	22 Jan 1874
Charles R. Darby	31 May 1878
Mary J. Darby	31 Jul 1886
C. Brown	27 Nov 1889
William W. Darby	4 May 1893
Andrew C. Brown	27 Dec 1898
Henry L. Black	17 Aug 1900
William W. Darby	12 May 1914 [died 10 Dec 1932]
	4th class
Laura Anna Pyles	18 Feb 1933 [retired 31 May 1951]
Warner D. Wood	31 May 1951
Maggie E. Cooley	27 Mar 1952
	discontinued, mail to Dickerson,
	31 May 1960
Mrs. C. Edgar Knill	had a post office station in her house on Ridge Rd. [now called Peachtree] which closed August 31, 1963. The area is now served by a rural carrier from Dickerson.

Mail was delivered by contract carriers in private cars to Poolesville, Beallsville and Barnesville. First class mail was hung on cranes by the railroad four times daily for pick-up. The carrier to Barnesville met three local passenger trains daily, and picked up mail at the railroad station. The Sellman Postmaster had to meet all train deliveries six days a week including all holidays.

The area which became Sellman was previously a farming community of rolling countryside with limited access. Some of the early residents c. 1814 were: William Darne, Dr. Samuel Newton Chiswell White, William Poole, Abraham S. Hayes, William Bennett, Brook Jones, Francis C. Clopper, Joseph I. Johnson, Nathan Hempstone, Jacob Nicholls, Horatio Trundle, Hezekiah Trundle, Richard Harding, William Trail, Thomas C. Lannan, School Master, Rev. Thomas Green, Dr. Horatio Willson, William Willson and Rev. Basil Berry. W. T. R. Saffell, author and historian was born September 18, 1818 at "Knott's Place" two miles south of Barnesville.

In 1838 the area was opened up by way of the road to Monocacy Chapel as Beallsville was then known. This road was commissioned to facilitate mail routes, provide access to the chapel, and for voting at Medley's Hill. The new road passed through Stanislaus Knott's property.

In 1865 plans for the Metropolitan Branch of the Baltimore and Ohio railroad were laid out. The crucial section of the line was Parr's Ridge, where the trains would have to climb 297 feet in the six miles between Dickerson and Barnesville. Therefore, construction began first in Barnesville in 1866, with James Boyd as the construction foreman on this section of track. He lived in a long red house near the tracks, near where the first station was built. The single track, 60 lb. John Brown rail, was a 1.1% grade for the trains to climb Parr's Ridge. In 1871 James and Ann Carlisle's land was purchased for the railroad bridge. The land taken from W. W. Darby split his farm in half. The crew also built the station house which was designed by E. Francis Baldwin. The same design was used at four other stations built during that decade. A second station was built closer to Barnesville which opened on November 16, 1906. Barnesville also had a siding track.

Train service began in Barnesville Station on May 25, 1873. The Sellman family had life rights to be the station master, but none of them ever were. The community around Barnesville Station was called Sellman in honor of William O. Sellman. The original schedule shows four passenger trains a day each way and three western expresses: one local, one Washington freight and one one-way freight. in 1874 an express was added that made the 42 mile trip to Point of Rocks in one hour and twenty minutes. The all-stops local took one hour and fifty minutes. By 1880 three through passenger trains and five freights, for a total of 14 passed by everyday. In more recent times five trains stopped here daily, three in the morning at 6:00, 7:00, and 9:45 AM and two in the evening at 6:00 and 7:00 PM.

Darby Road was commissioned in 1874 to provide access to the railroad and named it for Samuel Darby, Judge of the Orphan's Court. This is the current Peachtree Road. The road was extended in 1879 toward Thompson's Corner.

Sellman was a thriving commercial district, with mills, stores, a corn canning factory and cattle pens for holding stock delivered to be fattened on corn before slaughter.

Samuel Darby was the express agent in Sellman beginning in 1880. He owned and operated a store here. Nearby William B. White also had a shop. By 1882 the population of Sellman was 50. This included a postmaster, shoemaker, storekeepers, laborers, and a blacksmith. The Maryland Directory lists the following information about Sellman in 1882: "It is 17 miles from Rockville, land fair, sells for $50.00 an acre, produces 20 bushels wheat, 30 corn 1,000 lbs. tobacco and two tons hay. There is a church and school."

In 1912 the canning factory was established by Thomas & Co., Adamstown, also known as the Adamstown Canning and Supply Company plant on the east side of Sellman Station, and the north side of Sellman Rd. They also owned a mill beside the railroad station.

In 1919 Standard Oil Co. was founded adjacent to the tracks with J. R. Lillard as manager. In 1920 a new railroad station was built one quarter mile west of the former station. The 1906 station became the Pyles Store in 1923. The Metropolitan branch was so successful that a double track was laid in 1928 to allow for two way traffic. This eliminated many of the switches and long waits for passing trains.

The "Queen City" was the popular late morning train often used by the ladies to have an outing in Washington, to shop, have lunch and return on the evening train with their purchases mailed to arrive the next day. James Richard Nutter was the conductor for many years.

The Canning factory had an explosion in 1925. A pressure cooker tank was blamed for the tragedy in which several people were hurt and four were killed. The Watkins Cabinet Co. is now on this site.

After the heyday of the railroad, the third station sat abandoned. It was demolished in 1950. But the county did not anticipate the commuter traffic that would move into the area. On October 10, 1977 the former meter station of the Washington Gas Light Co. was moved to the MARC train stop in Sellman. The meter station had been scheduled for demolition, but has now been in service for 22 years in this location.

Chapter Four
Residences and Buildings

1. Wood House

William B. White lived here and was a rural mail carrier. The back part of the house is log, with a dirt cellar. The Wood family moved here in 1937. Hazel Wood Garvey sold to Julia and David Wise in 1967, and they sold it to John and Jill Crocker and it is presently being renovated by David Johnson.

2. Johnson-White House

The rear log section was constructed by William Thomas Johnson and the front Gothic Revival section was built in 1870. The architectural features of this house include a center gable, over round arched window in a steeply pitched roof. In 1889 it sold to Winfield Rice, who sold to William B. White. In 1902 Oscar K. Poole operated a general store across the street from this 84 acre parcel. Edward Barr ran the store for a while, and had a wagon with spices, vanilla and a variety of items that he took house to house through the country. Mr. Fletcher lived here and ran the store from the 1920's until the store burned down in 1936. A block building was erected for Carroll Lee Dickinson who lived there and ran the store. George Chastain operated for a short period of time after that.

3. site of Irving Thomas-Dorian P. Darne Mill

The granary and mill were built c. 1897 on the north side of the track. A siding provided space for cars waiting to be coupled to trains. Corn was shelled here and cobs were used for kindling, stove fuel, and privies. Green cobs were put out for hogs to root through. A road went behind the mill to the cattle pens which were used for stock being shipped by rail. Farmers also unloaded grain and corn to be milled and put into sacks. The mill was near an embankment, and the scales were located at the bottom of the hill. Feed was shipped out in railroad cars including bran, chicken feed, dairy feed, and mixes with proteins and minerals. Several silos were used in the storage of feed. The main floor of the mill was about four feet above ground to be level with railroad cars. The machinery was in the basement. Portable ramps were used to load grain from the mill to the railroad cars. Another building housed the office and sales area for farm tools, hardware, and wire. Irving Thomas and Co. owned the mill until it was sold to Dorian P. Darne in 1933. Hatton Brown managed the mill in early 1930's and two assistants worked there. Car loads of coal were unloaded here to be distributed to local customers for fuel. Tom Mossburg helped in the granary, Ellis Dayhoff worked in the mill, and Catherine Darne worked in the office. Mr. Darne was hooking up machinery one night in 1939 and sparks must have smoldered for several hours before the mill was engulfed in flames. The silos were all that were left. Recently the land sold for additional commuter parking at the MARC station and the last remains of the mill site were obliterated.

4. site of telegraph office

The telegraph office, which also housed the switching devices for the track, was built in 1906, when the double tracking of Parr's Ridge was completed. Clarence Warfel and Mr. Phillips were two of the telegraph operators here. The depot was also built in 1906 and opened on November 16. It was designed by E. Francis Baldwin and became the "standardized" design used at Washington Grove and many other stations. Because of the bottleneck created by the 1.1% grade on this section, it was the first to be double tracked.

5. Barnesville Station

The first depot, built in 1876, is shown in the photo along with the Poole children from Glen Ellen, 1902. Rear Left: Mabel Reeves, Mary Poole, Kitty Poole, Willson C. Poole, and Mabel Poole. The 1906 station was built closer to the commercial district. The Washington Meter Station that was moved to this location was built in the 1930's and was scheduled for demolition before being moved. With the increased use of MARC service, the parking lot for commuters was recently increased.

6. Warfel's Store

This structure was previously Clarence O. Warfel's Store. The two-story, three bay frame building was on land purchased in 1897 from Charles Early. There was a front porch and steps that have been gone for some time. It was converted into a residence for Mr. White and is now vacant.

7. Frank Gibson's House

Built for Henry White, this house was later owned by Frank Gibson, time keeper for the canning factory, and then was a rental property for many years. Frank Whisman lived here and in more recent years Mr. Gravely remodeled the house.

8. Dayhoff House

Mr. Dayhoff worked for the Thomas Canning Factory and moved here after the factory closed. Ellis, Bob, Douglas, Margaret and Louise were his children. John A. Jones, Jr. and then G. Max Lloyd lived here. It is presently a rental property.

9. Mt. Zion Parsonage

The parsonage was built in 1916 by James Cole, George and Charles Claggett and the men of Mt. Zion Church. Local trees were cut down and hauled to the sawmill for the lumber used in constructing the house. The parsonage was remodeled in 1964, while Reverend George Allen resided there. At that time an addition was built in the rear of the house.

10. Sellman School

The first school on this site was built c. 1866. It had a pot bellied stove and two blackboards and was located near the present church cemetery. One of the teachers was Miss Rachel Miller. In 1883 insurance on the school house was cancelled when it was discovered that the building was not owned by the county. In 1894 $425 was appropriated for the half acre lot and new one-room schoolhouse, which was subsequently insured. The lot was purchased from Algernon Poole. An addition was constructed in 1938 with Rhees E. Burkett appointed architect for Sellman School and a second room was added at this time. The contract went to S. F. Grimes for $4,469. In 1949 a contract was awarded to John Green for three wells at a cost of $1,279.00. In 1952, control of the building was given to The Women's Society of Mount Zion Methodist Church. In 1954 the building was sold to M-NCPP for $1.00 for park and recreational use. The building was no longer standing by 1972. Some of the teachers who taught here include Mrs. Gaither, Hazel Greene, Mary Johnson, Nina Clarke, Evelyn Hood, Samuel Jones and Mr. Waters.

11. Mt. Zion Wesleyan Methodist Church and Cemetery

The land where the church and cemetery are located were purchased by Philip Spencer from James O. and Annie E. Trundle. The old meeting house was located on land that is now the cemetery of the Mt. Zion Church, and was also used as a schoolhouse. The present congregation was founded in 1867. In 1883 a public school was constructed and used as the church on Sundays. In 1888 the cornerstone for a frame church building was laid. The vestibule and bell tower were added in 1937. The educational building was constructed in 1964, and the exterior of the church was bricked, and an addition was built.

Pastors of Mt. Zion:
Elijah P. Awkard		Luther Brown
C. H. Arnold		George Allen
James S. Cole		Washington Murray
Reverend Roan	1924	Perlena Woolridge
John C. Norris		Odell and Alice Carr
Walter Williams	1928	Homer Bullett
Joseph Stemley	1937	Laurence K. Bropleh
Howard Wallace		Joan Coates 1998
William E. Lee	1959	

Sellman Community Center

12. Chambers —Telfair B. Dorsett House

Old colonial style white house with columns, was built by Chambers who also lived there, the Hersbergers lived here in later years, followed by the Dorsetts in early 1940s. The living room in the center section of the house is very large, with a beautiful staircase to the left. When the kitchen was being modernized, the large windows left little wall space for appliances, but they give the house a grand and spacious appearance.

13. Boot Leg Hill

James Hallman lived in this house which reflects 1890's architecture. His son moved back to the area from Washington, DC and later lived here. There were several other occupants before the house was renovated in the 1960's by Edgar Grubb.

14. site of Glen Ellen

John Sprigg Poole was born in a house on this property in 1801. Part of tracts "Prospect Hill" and "Mt. Zion" the family called this "Pleasant Dale." There was a family cemetery here, however the stones have been moved to Monocacy Cemetery in Beallsville. One section of the house was built c. 1830 with several additions over the years. It was a frame Victorian House, two and a half stories on a fieldstone foundation. Glen Ellen burned in 1928. The present house was constructed on the old foundation for Willson Clark Poole. Willson Clark Poole, Jr. currently owns this farm and the house is occupied by his daughter, Mimi Poole Schultze and family.

15. J. R. Lillard's Standard Oil

James Robert Lillard distributed oil and kerosene from 1910-1930. Fuel was first hauled by mules and later by truck to customers. The land was leased by Samuel Creighton Jones in 1931 for Standard Oil of New Jersey and then in 1933 for Atlantic Refining Company. In later years this property was purchased by Mrs. Florence White Van Emon who later sold it to S. A. Carr who presently owns it and operates it under the name of S. A. Carr and Son Electrical Contractors.

16. Post Office and Store

The former railroad station, erected by the Baltimore and Ohio Railroad Co., became a store in 1923. John O. and Anna L. Pyles operated the store and W. W. Darby ran the post office which was located in the store. Following his death, Anna L. Pyles was the postmaster. Hatton D. Brown and W. W. Darby operated the feed store in back, and coal was also distributed from here. Boxcars were loaded and unloaded at this facility. The property was sold in 1952 to Roy Bedell who manufactured burial vaults at this location. S. A. Carr and Son subsequently purchased the property and combined it with their adjoining enterprise. Two interior shots of the store are on the following page.

17. Boyd House

Built in 1872, this building housed the construction crew and foreman Col. James A. Boyd for about a year. The house then became rental property owned by William Washington Darby. The house was referred to as "The Red House." Several families lived here including Homer Orme and James Robert Lillard when he was running the Standard Oil Co.

18. John O. Pyles House

The only house remaining on Sellman Road was built in 1916 by William Washington Darby. His daughter had moved to Kentucky with her husband John O. Pyles, and they decided to move back to Sellman. Their son, William Darby Pyles, was born there in 1916. Since 1952 this house has been rented to various people. Elsie Wood Pyles, wife of the late William D. Pyles is the present owner.

19. site of Canning Factory

The Adamstown Canning and Supply Co., built in 1912, was owned by Irving Thomas of Adamstown. Corn was the only product processed here, so the work was seasonal. Frank Gibson, the timekeeper, is pictured with his family. Corn was delivered to the factory in wagons pulled by four horse teams from area farms. After processing, it was shipped under several labels. In a pressure tank explosion a man named Copelin was scalded to death in 1926. The tragedy caused the end of the canning there, and the remains of the factory burned in 1938. The property was later sold to Wilbur and Jeannette Watkins and became part of the Watkins Cabinet Co., in 1967.

20. Thomas Canning Factory House

The house on the grounds of the Canning Factory was occupied by the Dayhoffs during the years that the factory was operating. Mr. Dayhoff did maintenance work during the off season. When the factory burned in 1938, this house burned to the ground also. This property was part of a four parcel purchase by Wilbur and Jeannette Watkins. It was purchased from Daily Knill on March 25, 1966.

The house which was beside the John O. Pyles house was that of William Washington Darby. Laura Anna Darby sold to S. P. Knill, who later sold to Jacob M. Johnson. After Richard Poole and Irma Brown purchased the house, they had it remodeled into three apartments. The house burned in April 21, 1971, Mr. and Mrs. William Baker, and Marco and Perlina Whismer perished in the blaze. Wilbur and Jeannette Watkins bought the property and incorporated it into the Watkins Cabinet Co.

22. Darby rental house

This house had only four rooms, two upstairs, and two downstairs. It was taken down to make room for the Watkins Cabinet Shop that was built in 1968.

23. Knott Farm

William Knott purchased "Conclusion" from John Belt and at his death in 1820 left the farm to his wife, Jane. His daughter Mary Ann was to receive the property after Jane's death. His son Edward received 122 acres and a house on that property, and the other children were to divide the remainder of the Knott land which adjoined Mr. Harding and Mrs. White. The farm house was two stories, and of frame construction, with several additions. The out buildings included a barn, machine shed, spring house, silo and other structures. The house is shown on the 1865 county map, and on the 1878 atlas, but it was gone by 1980.

24. Thomas F. Darne House

This Colonial Revival style house was built in the 1920's. It features a hipped roof, with dormers, a front porch and is two and a half stories. George Chastain sold it to Greydon Tolson, who currently lives here.

25. Thomas Mossburg House

When the Mossburg's purchased this property, the structure on it had been the Earp cabin. They remodeled the log cabin after the turn of the century. Mrs. Clara Mossburg sold this house in the 1930's. Several other families have lived here before Cliff Neal, the current owner, purchased the property.

Bibliography

Abstracts of Wills Mont. Co. 1776-1825
Backward Glance, Ida Lu Brown, 1988
Baltimore Sun, August 2, 1906
Baptist Church information by Laura Bennett
Civil War Guide to Montgomery County, Md., Charles T. Jacobs
From One Room to Open Space, E. Guy Jewell
Gaithersburg Gazette "Postal Service Day" by Jane Parsley, 1971
Genealogical Abstracts of The Sentinel 1855-1899, Montgomery County Historical Society
History of Montgomery County, T. H. S. Boyd
History of the Nineteenth-Century Black Churches in Maryland and Washington, DC, Nine Honemond Clarke, Vantage Press, 1981
Immpossible Challenge, Herbert H. Harwood, Jr., Barnard, Roberts and Co., Inc., Baltimore, Maryland
Interviews with Richard P. Brown
Interview with Nina Honemond Clarke, November 3, 1998
Interview with Idella Craven, November 9, 1998
Interview with Mike Dwyer, Montgomery Co. Parks Senior Historian
Interview with Dorothy Elgin, September, 1998
Interviews with Joe Elmer Hoyle
Interview with Frances Jones, June, 1998
Interview with Charles Knill, June 16, 1998
Interviews with J. Robert Lillard
Interviews with Jane Parsley
Interview with Susan Pignone, July 27, 1998
Interview with William Price, July, 1998
Interview with Elise Pyles, June 16, 1998
Interview with Louise Gott Ritchie, November 12, 1998
Interview with Mrs. Gordon Smith, September, 1998
Interview with Catherine Darne Stephens, September 18, 1998
Interview with Elizabeth Hays Tolbert, June 17, 1998
Interview with Rebecca Lillard Umstead, September, 1998
The Montgomery County Story, MCHS Aug 1872 vol. XV #4 Jane C. Sween
Post July 28, 1940 by Joseph M. Mathias "Oldest Resident of Barnesville"

Sentinel Newspaper March 28, 1896
Sugarloaf Regional Trails Research, 1970-1976
Towns of Montgomery County, Jane Sween "How Some of
 Montgomery Towns Received Their Name"
"Tidbit" Barnesville Newsletter, October 1998, Patty Menke
Washington Post, August 4, 1975
Washington Post, May 26 1982
Washington Post, May 22, 1988

Index

Abercrombie, John, 4
Alexander, William, 49
Allen, George, 119, 121
Ambush, Henry, 79, James, 20, Martha, 79, Mr., 36
Anderson, Hamilton, 57, John, 68 Larry, 68, Mrs., 50
Appleby, Mary, 45, Nicholas, 45
Arnold, C., 121
Ashby, Col. 7
Atwood, Barton, 16, Ella, 16
Austin, Thomas, 57
Awkard, Elijah, 121, Leonard, 11

B & O Railroad, 9, 131
Bailey, Woody, 96
Baker, Will, 47, William, 133
Baldwin, E. Francis, 109, 114
Baltimore Road, 1, 3, 46
Banks, Nathaniel, 4
Barnes, Ann, 30, James, 1, 30
Barnesville Academy, 9, 13, 98
Barnesville Baptist Church, 3, 9, 21, 24, 71, 82
Barnesville, Community Hall, 15, 74
Barnesville Guards, 4
Barnesville Grange, 10, 12, 14, 53, 85
Barnesville Methodist Church, 11, 21, 46, 50
Barnesville School, 21, 66, 80, 85
Barnesville Station, 9
Barr, Bryan, 14, 91, Cherry, 75, 97, Donald, 91,

Barr, Edward, 112, Estelle, 91, George, 15, Mary, 91
Battle of Antietam, 4
Battle of Bladensburg, 2
Beagle, Glen, 35
Beall, Lemuel, 57
Beall, Upton, 2
Beallsville, 25, 104, 109
Bean, William, 19
Beatty, Warren, 16
Bedell, Roy, 127
Bell, Avery, 57, Isaac, 49
Belt, John, 134, Richard, 57
Bennett, William, 109
Benson, Daniel, 23, Don, 54
Berry, Basil, 109
Bethel Chapel, 3, 50, 56
Bifield, James, 39
Birch, Joseph, 37, 38, 40, 41
Black, Henry, 108
Borgnay, P., 38
Boyd, James, 112, 131
Boyle, T., 39
Bowlen, George, 5, 10, 12, 21, 35, 41, 58, Mary, 58
Bowman, Frederick, 20
Boyd, James, 9, 109, 129
Boyle, T. E., 38
Bready, Arthur, 15, 81, Helen, 15, 81
Brewer, Ruth, 106, Stephen, 20, 102
Bropleh, Laurence, 121
Brosius, Charles, 14, 39, 62, Jarboe, 39
Brown, Andrew, 108, Bonnie, 69, Bub, 68, C., 108, Charles, 75, Clarence, 77, Clark, 69,

Brown, Deborah, 49, Emily, 19, 47, Hatton, 20, 49, 54, 58, 88, 117, 127, Ida Lu, 17, 32, 106, Irma, 137, John, 4, 9, 11, 12, 14, 19, 21, 52, 55, 56, 57, 58, Luther, 121, Maisie, 80, Philip, 20, 39, Richard, 20, 60, 85, 136, 137, Sallie, 4, 6, 14, 19, 20, Thomas, 25, 68, William, 4, 14, 15, 47, 52, 55
Bruner, Mac, 95, 96
Bullett, Homer, 121
Burdette, C., 80
Burner, Carl, 100, Mary, 95
Burke, E., 83
Burkett, Rhees, 120
Bushby, William, 104
Butke, Loretta, 81, William, 81
Butt, Ernest, 51
Byrd, Marjory, 35

Callear, James, 55, Mildred, 55
Carlin, John, 12, 21
Carlisle, Ann, 109, David, 6, James, 109, William, 6
Carr, Alice, 121, Odell, 121, S. A., 126, 131, W., 10
Carroll, Michael, 38
Ceadell, H., 80
Cecil, Clara, 66, 80, Daisy, 66, 80, Luther, 11, 12, 13, 21, 64, 66, Murrell, 66, Oscar, 70
C. & O. Canal, 3, 9, 40
Chandler, Hartwell, 50
Chapman, Robert, 56
Chastain, George, 112, 135
Chiswell, Edward, 52
Christ Episcopal Church, 6, 11, 21, 99, 108
Claggett, Bessie, 76,

Claggett, Charles, 12, 73, 76, 80, 119, Earl, 80, George, 76, 119, Sarah, 2, 69
Clarksburg, 71, 81
Clarke, Nina, 120
Clopper, Francis, 109
Coates, Joan, 121
Coberth, David, 6
Cole, David, 25, James, 119, 121
Coleman, James, 83
Collins, Stewart, 80
Comus, 4, 66, 81
Cooley, C. G., 20, 71, George, 20, Harold, 20, 74, Jack, 16, 20, 33, Maggie, 108, Nellie, 74, Ralph, 16, Zachariah, 20
Cooper, Herbert, 83
Cotter, Tinker, 45
Coughlin, John, 11, 12, 21, 92
Cowell, F., 83
Cox, E., 56
Criswell, Leah, 82
Crocker, Jill, 111, John, 111
Crook, Guy, 104
Crowley, Brad, 87, Glenda, 87
Cuddy, J., 39, Michael, 38
Cunningham, Mrs., 14

Darby, Charles, 14, 82, 111, Ed, 102, J., 20, Jim, 15, John, 10, Laura, 108, 131, 137, Mary, 82, 103, 108, R., 10, Reginald, 103, Samuel, 82, 110, William, 82, 108, 109, 127, 129, 134, 133
Darne, Catherine, 113, Dorian, 113, Thomas, 135, William, 109, 117
Davidson, Dalis, 102
Davis, Notley, 16, William, 83
Day, J. Edward, 56

Dayhoff, Douglas, 118, Ellis, 113, 122, Louise, 118, Margaret, 118, Mr. 118, 135, 136
DeFries, Jeddie, 83 Lorraine, 83
DeVos, P., 38, 39
Dickerson, 6, 17, 38, 43, 51, 108, 109
Dickinson, Carroll, 112
Digges, Edward, 3
Dixon, Charles, 69, Eberly, 69, 83, Herbert, 14, 15, 19
Donaldson, Jesse M., 16
Dorrsett, Telfair, 123
Dougherty, William, 3
Driscoll, Francis, 39
Dubois, Edith, 83, Horace, 83, John, 2, 37
Dudley, Mrs., 96
Duvall, Matilda, 44

Eagle, Lycurgus, 34, Sarah, 12, 34
Earle, Sydney, 42
Early, Charles, 116
Easter, 16, Albert, 20, Mrs., 70
Edelin, Eleanor, 49, James, 49
Edward's Ferry, 6
Elder, Ira, 2
Elkins, 100
Ellis, Mr., 5
Erlich, Carol, 16, Paul, 16, 100
Erp, Burgess, 2

Farnsworth, John, 5
Farr, Sharon, 56
Feaster, Elizabeth, 49, Jacob, 49
Finn, Michael, 100
Fink, Walter, 101
Fitch, Fanny, 35, 62,

Fitch, James, 35, 62, Tim, 63, William, 6
Fischer, Diane, 44, Walter, 44
Fisher, Frances, 90, Spencer, 20, 90, William, 33
Fitsimmons, Lucy, 81
Fleming, Thomas, 83
Flinn, H. Marvin, 83
Foley, Thomas, 38
Fouth, Mrs. 35
Fowler, Charles, 47, 49, Frank, 48
Franklin, Gen., 4
Funk, George, 89

Gaither, Mrs. 120
Gallagher, M. P., 38
Ganley, James, 38
Garver, Nellie, 77
Garvey, Hazel, 111
Getzendanner, Annie, 12
Gibson, Frank, 117, 131
Gittings, Edward, 65
Gleeson, James, 1, 2, 31
Gloyd, John, 38
Gott, Ethel, 98, J. Forrest, 15, 72, 98, John, 19, 52, Laura, 82, Richard, 2
Gormley, Harry, 39
Gough, Gertrude, 19
Gouillot, Paul, 44
Gravely, Mr. 117
Green, John, 6, 124, Thomas, 109
Greene, Hazel, 120
Griffith, E., 82, F., 82, Jemima, 82, Mr., 5, 49, Prudence, 26
Griffiths, B., 104
Griggs, W., 104
Grimes, Gassway, 57, S. 120

Grubb, Lloyd, 124
Gue, Lindell, 49

Hall, H., 83
Haller, Robert, 20, 31
Hallman, Arthur, 91, Cora, 91, James, 124
Hamilton, Alex, 112, Gen., 4
Harding, Abraham, 6, Mr., 136, 138, Richard, 109
Hargett, Margie, 80
Harrington, George, 38
Harris, Abraham, 20, 52, 53, Joseph, 3, 56, Mary, 56, S., 20, Sarah, 82, Wilhelmina, 49
Harwood, Henrietta, 57
Hatcher, Hilleary, 83
Hawse, Albert, 16
Hawkins, Peter, 2, Elizabeth, 49, Mary, 66
Hays, Abraham, 1, 3, 63, 80, 109, Bettie, 65, Edward, 57, Eleanor, 53, Eliza, 50, 85, 104, Elizabeth, 53, 104, F., 15, 72, Fred, 12, 13, 16, 20, 52, 80, 85, 99, George, 2, 52, Ida, 13, 80, 85, 90, 104, Jeremiah, 1, 63, John, 49, L., 20, Leonard, 2, 3, 10, 11, 12, 14, 19, 27, 30, 31, 46, 49, 52, 53, 61, 63, 65, 85, Martha, 57, R., 16, 20, Richard, 4, 6, 10, 12, 21, 28, 64, 65, 118, Samuel, 6, 12, 19, 21, 44, Sarah, 57, Thomas, 50, William, 30, 33
Hays School, 44, 59, 94
Hayes, Anna, 53, Samuel, 53, Sarah, 53, William, 19
Hempstone, Nathan, 109
Henderson, John, 6
Hersberger, Arthur, 15, 63, 72,

Hersberger, Milton, 15, Mrs., 20, Rosalyn, 15
Hershey, Christian, 20, 57, David, 57, John, 57
Hess, Carl, 39
Hickerson, Henry, 94
Hildebrand, Mae, 97
Hill, Clifton, 58, Doris, 58
Hilliard, Thomas, 90
Hilton, Clagett, 12, 13, 14, 15, 31, 35, 46, 72, 92, 94, F., 82, John, 25, 33, 35, 64, Lonnie, 15, 96, Mortimer, 35, 83, Sedonia, 88, William, 4, 6, 9,10, 11, 12, 13, 15, 20, 24, 27, 32, 33, 36, 38, 61, 82, 90, 92, 94, 104
Hodges, Benjamin, 94, William, 20
Holland, Horace, 49
Hood, Evelyn, 120
Horton, Hazel, 85
Howard, Eleanor, 49, Elisha, 49
Hoyle, Arthur, 41, Elmer, 56, Joseph, 39, 56
Hurley, William, 3
Hyattstown, 81
Hyland, Martin, 39

Jameson, Virgie, 91
Jamison, Alexander, 12, Fr., 38
Jay, King, 57, Stephen, 57
Jeffers, Benton, 15, Donald, 15 Julia, 21, 81, Mark, 15, 20, Paul, 15 85, Richard, 15, 85
Jeffrey, Pat, 75
Johnson, David, 32, 61, 111, Edwin, 31, Jacob, 137, Joseph, 109, John, 14, 15, 80, Mary, 120, Thomas, 57,

142

Johnson, William, 116, 118
Jones, Ann, 38, Benjamin, 6,
  Beulah, 39, Brook, 109,
  Charles, 78, Ellen, 57, Fred,
  14, Isaac, 52, J., 49, John, 12,
  21, 52, 123, Joseph, 82, 87,
  Leonidas, 52, Lewis, 83,
  Lillian, 39, Lizzie, 82, Lloyd,
  5, 10, 38, Mary, 25, 78,
  Mercer, 39, Mollie, 4, Samuel,
  120, 126, Sarah, 38, W. 39
Jordan, E. Wilson, 20, 71

Kacacharow, Eugene, 99
Kessler, Herbert, 20, 58, Mary,
  58, Tom, 15
Kinder, John, 30
King, F., 38
Kingsbury, Mrs., 38, 39
Kittleman, Laura, 95
Kleinstuber, Joseph, 39
Knill, Daily, 132, C. Edgar, 108,
  Mary, 16, S. P., 137
Knott, Edward, 134, Francis,
  11, 13, 73, Jane, 134, Mary
  Ann, 134, Mary Jane, 12,
  43, 71, 137, Mrs., 21,
  Stansilaus, 109, William, 134,
  Zachariah, 1, 37, 38, 137

Lacy, Dr., 5, 49
Lafferty, C., 104
Lankford, Mary, 90, William, 90
Lannan, Thomas, 57, 109
Lawless, Deaner, 16, Margaret,
  16
Lawman, Charles, 20, James, 20
Layton, Uriah, 5
Lee, Robert, 4, W., 27,
  William, 121

Leonard, Thomas, 38
Lillard, E., 15, Bobby, 15,
  James Robert, 14, 15, 20, 24,
  25, 66, 67, 68, 110, 126, 129,
  Marjorie, 66, Stella, 19, 66
Linthicum, Frederick, 20
Lisle, Dr., 2
Littell, Tilly, 45
Little Monocacy Creek, 82
Lloyd, G., 118, Zachariah, 2
Lodge, J., 83
Loy, Julia, 11, 12, Zack, 14, 43
Luhn, Ethel, 85, June, 16, Randy,
  15, Todd, 16
Lynch, John, 20

Maguire, J., 38
Manion, James, 12, 42, Kiernon,
  13, 14, 20, 42
Marsh, John, 83
Maryland Militia, 4
Matthews, Doris, 16, Evelyn,
  19, Walter, 10
Maus, Oliver, 11, 12
McAbee, Hester, 49, John, 49
McClellan, Robert, 4
McDonald, George, 38, Gilbert,
  38, Patrick, 14
McFadden, J. C., 14, 83
McGaha, Archie, 16
McGary, Mr. 57
McLaughlins, 43
McManus, Fr., 38
Meany, Miss, 81
Meissner, Paul, 90, Scott,
  101, Trudy, 90
Menke, Dorothy, 77, George,
  77, 81, John, 81, Meg, 81,
  Peter, 70
Merrel, G., 71

Miles, Charles, 10, Elisha, 11,
Miles, Elisha, 12, George, 35,
Miles, Nathan, 10, 35, 42
Millburn, L., 83
Miller, George, 98, Houston, 102, Rachel, 120
Mitchell, Robert, 43, Donna, 43
Moon, Lowell, 103
Monocacy aqueduct, 1
Monocacy Chapel, 112
Monocacy River, 3, 94, 93
Moomaw, Carol, 15
Morgan, Rev., 50
Morningstar, Algie, 20, 48, Archie, 43, Claudia, 43, Edgar, 20, 44, Edna, 49, James, 49, Mary, 20, 61, 80, Tom, 15
Mosby, William, 4
Mossburg, Clara, 136, Thomas, 100, 113, 136
Moulden, Elias, 6, 65, 92, Mary, 65
Mouth of Monocacy, 33, 45
Murphy, Caroline, 57, Joseph, 30, Mr., 3, Randolph, 3, William, 65
Murray, Washington, 121
Myers, William, 99

Neal, Cliff, 136
Nichols, Charles, 10, 12, 20, G., 48, Jacob, 49, 50, 63, 109, Martha, 53, Mary, 57, Sarah, 49, 50, Thomas, 57
Nicholson, Burt, 61, Carrie, 61
Nicoll, H., 83
Norris, John, 121
Noyes, Alfred, 17, 103
Nutter, James, 110

Oakland Mills, 46
O'Boyle, Patrick, 39
Oden, Rachel, 82
Offutt, Clarence, 60, Colmore, 49, L. Jerome, 16, 39, 49, 62, Leonard, 58, 62, Mary A., 49, Mary L., 19, 62
O'Meara, Claire, 88
O'Neil, Bernard, 1, 37
Orme, Anne, 62, Allen, 12, 19, 21, 32, 92, Charles, 15, 20, Henry, 6, Homer, 129, Lindly, 6, Maurice, 31, 46
Owens, R., 83

Painter, Elmer, 97, Jim, 83
Parsley, James, 95, Jane, 95
Pateros, Pat, 98, Peg, 98
Pearcy, Glen, 100, Susan, 100
Phillips, Milton, 15, 74
Pearre, Catherine, 57, George, 57, James, 20, 57, John, 30, Mary, 57, William, 57
Pepe, Victor, 45
Perlmeter, Alan, 71
Phillips, Algie, 97, Bryan, 96, Mary, 96, Milton, 72, 97
Pignone, Susan, 60, Tom, 60
Piles, Thomas, 76
Pinckney, William, 104
Plummer, John, 1, 2, 44, 60, Mary, 50, 57, Philemon, 49, 57, Sarah, 49, 50, Solomon, 11, 12, 21, 44
Plunkett, Father, 1
Piles, Thomas, 80
Pinckney, William, 108
Pipe Creek, 1
Poole, Agernon, 20, 120, E., 12, Ellen, 31, Green, 14, John, 2, 30, 33, 12, 85, 86, 125,

144

Poole, Kitty, 115, Mabel, 115, Mary, 28, 119, Oscar, 97, 98, 99, 100, 116, Priscilla, 12, 65, 86, Richard, 28, Thomas, 30, William, 15, 19, 109, Willson, 115, 125
Poolesville, 6, 9, 81, 88, 104, 108
Pormellown, Sarah, 65
Price, Daniel, 45, Deborah, 87, Ida Lu, 16, 17, 19, Jane, 16, Jessie, 33, Lawrence, 14, 15, 20, 33, 87, William, 75, 97
Pumphrey, Robert, 58
Pyles, Anna, 127, Elsie, 130, F., 19, Isaac, 13, 21, 62, John, 131, 134, 133, Laura, 50, 111, Percy, 14, Rebecca, 62, Richard, 11, 13, 19, 21, 50, 61, Thomas, 61, William, 130

Ray, Eleanor, 81
Redmond, James, 38
Reeves, Mabel, 115
Reid, Alousius, 38, Ann, 39, 95, George, 30, 39, 90, Sarah, 38, Thomas, 2, W., 20, William, 38, 39
Renshaw, Eloise, 80
Reynolds, L., 38
Rice, R. Alonzo, 13, 30
Ricketts, Maurice, 30, 68
Riordan, M., 38, 40
Ritchie, Joseph, 39, 41
Roan, Rev., 121
Roberson, Benjamin, 13, 43, 51
Rockville, 2, 9
Rogers, Mr., 57
Rosser, General, 6
Ruhl, Robert, 88
Ryman, Harold, 15, Homer, 51

Saffell, W., 109
Savage, Harry, 89
Scholls, G. 48, John, 6
Schultze, Mimi, 125
Sears, John, 63
Sedwick, William, 2
Sellman, Ann, 82, 86, Charles, 90, Henry, 6, L., 20, John, 20, 57, Richard, 86, William O., 2, 3, 28, 57, 82, 86, 109
Shannon, Mr., 70
Shaver, S., 83
Shaw, V., 94
Shears, George, 104
Sheehan, Jacquelin, 58, William, 58
Sherman, Wilhelmina, 13, 21, 51
Shipley, Walker, 49
Shoup, Mildred, 72, William, 83
Shreve, Daniel, 39, Earl, 16, Margaret, 39
Siegel, Bernard, 39
Slackman, Joel, 63
Smith, A., 104, Charles, 65, Gordon, 100, John, 50, Mary, 65, R., 83
Spencer, Charles, 80, Philip, 121
Sprigg, Frederick, 86, Priscilla, 86
Spriggs, Samuel, 2
Spruyt, H., 38, 41
St. John's Church, 1, 38
St. Mary's Church, 3, 4, 5, 9, 10, 15, 16, 37, 39, 40
Stallings, Richard, 6
Starkey, Joseph, 15
Staub, Charles, 50
Stemley, Joseph, 121
Stevens, Paul, 81

Stevens, Paul, 81
Stiers, Jacob, 2, 43
Stonestreet, Dr., 14, Joseph, 65, Robert, 65, Virginia, 65
Story, Edward, 88, Thomas, 10, 13, 80, 88, 94
Stottlemyer, Harold, 20, 31
Stowers, John, 15
Stuart, J. E. B., 4, 5, 6, 7, 27
Sugarloaf Mountain, 3, 4, 5, 7, 17, 23, 24, 36, 57, 62, 87
Sullivan, J., 38

Talbott, Joseph, 3, Nathan, 6, 9, 10, 13, 21, 35, 59, 60, 70, 75, 78, 88, 94
Tankersley, Mrs., 85
Taylor, Martin, 6
Thomas, Beverly, 68, 86, Henry, 104, Irving, 113, 117, 134, Sallie, 86
Thompson, Major, 6, Richard, 57
Tillard, Edward, 1, 2
Titus, Edna, 19
Tolbert, Elizabeth, 17, 23, 27, 44, Samuel, 15, 44
Tolson, Greydon, 135
Torrey, Julia, 76, Mark, 76
Trail, Abigail, 50, 65, Frances, 57, Jane, 57, Mortimer, 57, Oscar, 57, William, 2, 50, 109
Trundle, Annie, 120, Elizabeth, 53, Hezekiah, 109, Horatio, 112, James, 120, John, 54
Tucker, Benjamin, 2
Tyson, Winifred, 41

Van Emon, Antoinnette, 44, Carlton, 20, 44, Florence, 126

Veatch, Nathan, 2, 54,
Veatch, Thomas, 72
Von Dem Busche, Carl, 15, 103
Vorhees, A., 20

Wade, Alice, 50, Carson, 92, Courtney, 81, Harriet, 50, 63, James, 50, Mary, 50, Thomas, 82
Wagner, P. 83
Wailes, Captain, 27
Wallace, Howard, 121
Ward, Barbara, 16, Carson, 85, 88, Charles, 16, Courtney, 84, Gigi, 32, Harry, 32, Silas, 2, Thomas, 78
Warfel, Clarence, 114, 116, Elsie, 86
Warfield, William, 3
Warren, Howard, 75, William, 20
Waters, Mr. 120
Watkins, Jeannette, 131, 133, 137, Wilbur, 131, 133, 137
Webster, Daniel, 27, Fletcher, 27, Maureen, 19, 35, 106, Paul, 35
Welker, Blaine, 83
Whalen, Millard, 13
Whisman, Frank, 117, Mr., 137
Whismer, Marco, 133, Perlina, 133
White, Benjamin, 50, 52, Eleanor, 56, Henry, 121, Howard, 118, Hulda, 13, Joseph, 14, 63, Laura, 90, Mary, 13, 21, 63, 82, Mrs., 137, Richard, 31, 82, S., 83, Samuel, 109, Sarah, 50, Thomas, 13, 14, 90, W.

White, William, 101, 110, 111, 116
White's Ford, 4, 5
Williams, Lieut., 5, Otho, 1, Walter, 121
Willson, Horatio, 109, William, 109
Wilson, James, 20
Winsor, Arnold, 3
Wise, David, 111, Julia, 111
Wolfe, Annie, 35, 82 Joel, 35, 43, 82, 118
Wood, George, 16, 73, Georgianna, 73, Gertrude, 65, Robert, 10, 13, 21, 25, 65 Warner, 108
Woolridge, Perlena, 121
Wothen, Gabriel, 62
Wotton, Albert, 98
Wrede, Connie, 70
Wright, James, 83
Wroth, E., 104
Wyatt, Robert, 91

Yeatts, Tom, 95
Yohn, Dr., 100
Young, Issac, 52, Miss, 85
Yost, Caleb, 50

Zeigler, F., 11, G., 11

Other Heritage Books by Dona L. Cuttler:

Montgomery Circuit Records, 1788-1988 [Maryland]

One Man's Family

Paperclips: Selected Clippings from The Montgomery Sentinel *[Maryland], 1900-1950*

The Cemeteries of Hyattstown [Maryland]

The Genealogical Companion to Rural Montgomery Cemeteries.

The History of Barnesville and Sellman, Maryland
Dona L. Cuttler and Ida Lu Brown

The History of Clarksburg, King's Valley, Purdum, Browningsville and Lewisdale [Maryland]

The History of Dickerson, Mouth of Monocacy, Oakland Mills, and Sugarloaf Mountain [Maryland]

The History of Comus [Maryland]

The History of Hyattstown [Maryland]

The History of Poolesville [Maryland]
Dona L. Cuttler and Dorothy J. Elgin

ABOUT THE AUTHOR

Dona L. Cuttler is a Maryland native who descended from several pre-colonial Maryland family lines. She is a graduate of Takoma Academy, and USC. Her great-grandfather and grandmother started the family interest in genealogy, and local history, and Ms. Cuttler has expanded the project throughout several counties in Maryland.

www.ingramcontent.com/pod-product-compliance
Lightning Source LLC
Chambersburg PA
CBHW040318170426
43197CB00021B/2950